MYTHS AND LEGE[N]

THE WAR OF HORUS AND SET

AUTHOR: DAVID McINTEE

ILLUSTRATOR: MARK STACEY

First published in Great Britain in 2013 by Osprey Publishing,
Midland House, West Way, Botley, Oxford, OX2 0PH, UK
44–02 23rd St, Suite 219, Long Island City, NY 11101, USA
E-mail: info@ospreypublishing.com

Osprey Publishing is part of the Osprey Group

A CIP catalog record for this book is available from the British Library

Print ISBN: 978 1 780967226
PDF e-book ISBN: 978 1 780967226
EPUB e-book ISBN: 978 1 78200 330 4

Typeset in Garamond Pro and Myriad Pro

Originated by PDQ Media, Bungay, UK
Printed in China through Asia Pacific Offset Limited.

13 14 15 16 17 10 9 8 7 6 5 4 3 2 1

E-mail: customerservice@ospreypublishing.com

Osprey Publishing is supporting the Woodland Trust, the UK's leading woodland conservation
charity, by funding the dedication of trees.

www.ospreypublishing.com

CONTENTS

INTRODUCTION

Ancient Egypt is one of the most fascinating and popular subjects of study in the world, both in terms of its archaeology and its mythology. It has interested people for thousands of years. Even when the Ancient Greeks ruled Egypt as pharaohs, there was already an *Ancient* Egypt to look back on. The Pyramids were ancient mysteries even to these pharaohs, and the origins of the old stories and myths had long since been forgotten.

The Romans were similarly intrigued, as were the Arabs, the Crusaders, and the scientists and historians of Napoleon's army. Even today, television programmes about Ancient Egypt are immensely popular on the various documentary channels, perhaps only beaten by programmes on animals and UFOs.

Egypt's mythology, though sometimes forgotten and misunderstood, has always come back into popularity in some form. In particular, the story of Set, Horus, and the overthrow and resurrection of Osiris has survived for four and a half thousand years. It is a story that was not only among the most important for the Ancient Egyptians, but is one that still influences tales today. There are many reasons for this popularity and longevity, not least of which is that the rivalry between siblings is one of the most basic stories there is. Both in life and in fiction, everyone knows that brothers are as often rivals as they are allies, and so a story with that theme – such as that of Set and Horus – is truly universal. An audience does not need to be Egyptian to understand and empathize with it, and that makes it timeless.

This book retells this particular timeless story in modern words. It explains how the story developed over time, and also delves into the real-world events of Egyptian history that inspired and affected the myth.

(Opposite) A modern interpretation of Horus. (Artwork by Yigit Koroglu)

THE GODS AND THEIR REALM

The Creation of the World and the Gods

The feud between Set and Horus began long before Horus was born, when Set and Osiris were the first brothers born among the gods. Like many pantheons of gods around the world, the Egyptian gods started off as a single family, with the children, grandchildren, and great-grandchildren of the original creator, Atum.

At the very beginning, there was a void filled with only the primal waters of chaos, and this was called Nu. The only solid thing in the world – in fact the only thing in reality at all – was a pyramid-shaped rock called the Benben, and when the Egyptians later built actual pyramids, they topped them with carved Benben stones to represent this one, and sheathed those capstones in gold.

Then a very strange thing happened. The first god was sitting on the Benben stone. He didn't come *from* anywhere; he simply was there at that moment. The name given to him by the Egyptians, Atum, derives from the word meaning 'to complete', and so his name refers to the fact that he completed himself. This was only the beginning, however, and he had more creation to finish.

Atum finds that there's a serpent – Apep – in the chaos surrounding the world. (Universal Images Group / DeAgostini / Alamy)

Of course, Atum only had himself with which to create anything. The earliest version of the story is in the Pyramid Texts. These are spells carved and painted into the walls of pyramids' burial chambers from around the 5th Dynasty – 2400-2300 BC – which were intended to both protect and guide the pharaoh in his journey through the afterlife, as well as to persuade and threaten the gods into being favourable. Two hundred and twenty-eight spells were recorded, at the end of the 5th Dynasty, in the Pyramid of Unas at Saqqara. According to these, Atum sneezed out Shu, the god of the air, and spat out Tefnut, the goddess of water. In later, and ruder, versions, he created this first pair of siblings by means of a quite different bodily fluid.

The first thing that Shu and Tefnut did, like all good children, was leave home. They went off to explore the universe into which they had been born. Atum was distraught at the loss of his children, and so created fire, to light the way that led to them. Eventually, the message of fire found them, and they returned, making Atum so happy that he burst into tears. These tears fell upon the rock, where they became the first men.

Pyramid Texts? The clue's in the name: texts carved or painted inside pyramids. In this case, the burial chamber of Unas, last pharaoh of the 5th Dynasty, inside his pyramid at Saqqara. There are 228 spells carved into this lot. (The Art Archive / Alamy)

Shu and Tefnut, meanwhile, being the first male and female couple, had done what came naturally, and mated. As a result, Tefnut soon gave birth to a son and a daughter. The son, Geb, became the earth, and the daughter, Nut, became the heavens, in the form of the night sky. In turn, Geb and Nut became parents themselves, to two sons and two daughters. The sons were none other than Osiris and Set, and the daughters were Isis and Nephthys.

Both of Geb's sons would go on to be very famous in Egyptian mythology, and to have a lasting legacy, but the eldest son, Osiris, would have influence all the way to the present day. Geb's eldest son is still known today as Osiris, but there were some who called him by a different name at first. Some called him Horus, the same name that would be given to his own son, and insisted that he was therefore Horus the Elder, who only became Osiris when he went into the underworld to rule over it.

The Gods

Ancient Egypt had somewhere in the region of two thousand gods, and probably a lot more, if local town and village deities are included. Many of these gods, however, were actually just different names – and different regional attributes – for the same god or goddess. For example, the original unique self-created creator god was Atum, who first appeared on the Benben stone out of the chaotic waters of the void, and who created his children Shu and Tefnut from within himself alone. However, the original unique self-created creator god was also called Amun, who created his children with his third wife, Mut. She was his wife after Wosret and Amunet, who was the female side of himself! Mut, in turn, was also the original unique self-created creator goddess.

This is a big problem when trying to understand Egyptian mythology. So many of the gods share attributes and origin stories, so many have varying origin stories, and so many of the gods and goddesses are combined – like colours or flavours – into new forms in different periods. For example, Ra, the king of the gods, often has his name appended to both Atum and Amun, both of whom were the original king of the gods before being merged back with Ra later on.

In the case of Atum-Ra, he then fathered Shu and Tefnut upon Iusaaset, rather than on his own as the story was originally told. Iusaaset seems to have been his shadow, who split from Atum-Ra in a form of parthenogenesis in order to become the grandmother of the gods.

Ra in his solar barque, *Mandjet*. (The Print Collector / Alamy)

The reason for all of this is actually quite simple, even if the result is not. It is because Egypt was originally two kingdoms, and in fact was known to the Egyptians as The Two Lands. Upper and Lower Egypt's mythological developments were somewhat different, albeit always mixed together. So, while Atum founded the nine gods called the Ennead according to the religion based at Heliopolis in Lower Egypt, Amun and his wives founded a council of eight gods – called the Ogdoad – according to the religion that was based in the Upper Egyptian city of Thebes.

From this point onwards, both kingdoms shared many of the same gods, such as Ra, Thoth, Sekhmet and so on, as well as having local gods for local people. The gods could be larger than life, literally: the only surviving description says that on earth they were six cubits tall – about 4.3 metres, or over 15 feet – while Ra was a man one million cubits tall! In most artworks the gods are shown as man-size or slightly larger, however. Some sources also describe the gods as having golden skin in their full majesty, though other sources give the gods individual colours to represent attributes (for example, black for the fertility of the Nile Delta's soil, or green for rebirth and resurrection), and most are shown in paintings with normal Egyptian skin.

Before too long, the great family spread and expanded, and there were many more gods throughout Egypt. So, just who are the gods involved in this myth, and what sort of deities were they?

Cast of Gods

Ra

Ra was the Egyptian sun god, with the head of a falcon, the centre of whose worship was at Heliopolis. He was born from an egg (or a lotus flower) on the same Benben mound as Atum, and, like Atum, created man from his tears. While Atum is generally not mentioned in mythology after the creation story, Ra shares so many of his attributes – as creator, as a sun god, as leader of the council of the gods – that it is quite likely that they are in fact meant to be the same god. From the 2nd to the 4th dynasties, the sun god began to be called Ra, and sometime around the 5th Dynasty, about 2400 BC, the name of Atum was replaced by that of Ra, and sometimes combined with it as Atum-Ra.

Ra was therefore the chief god, and it was his responsibility to take the sun across the sky in his boat. It was also his responsibility to make sure the sun survived its journey through the Duat at night, and rose again in the morning. Ra was therefore an important god, well-loved and worshipped ever more spectacularly. He also had a dark side, though, and more than once decided to wipe out humanity. Ra had a paranoid streak, which sometimes made him fear that humanity was plotting to overthrow him. When he was in these moods, he would send his daughters, Hathor and Sekhmet, to wipe out the human race. Luckily Hathor was a fertility goddess, and more interested in breeding humans than killing them, so she would brew red beer to make Sekhmet the lioness sleepy when she drank it in the belief that it was blood, and dance for Ra until his mood calmed.

Ra's name was also sometimes combined with that of Horus, but not the Horus who would fight Set. In order to cast Ra as supreme ruler of both the daylight world of life and the underworld of night and death, the title Ra-Horakhty (Horus of the Two Horizons) linked him with Osiris, ruler of the underworld, who was also called Horus the Elder.

Osiris

Osiris was the eldest son of Geb and Nut, and was said to be the original pharaoh. He was the god of the Nile and of resurrection. After his death, he became the king of the underworld and merciful judge of the dead. He is usually shown as a bandaged mummy, with either green skin (as the colour of resurrection and rebirth) or black skin (as the god of the fertile soil of the Nile Delta).

Despite quickly becoming the central figure of Egyptian funerary texts, and so important to the whole culture of death, rebirth, and apotheosis of the pharaoh, the earliest mention of Osiris is from the 5th Dynasty, when tomb paintings suddenly began to show the deceased pharaoh making offerings to him instead of to Anubis, as had previously been the case. Prior to this, Anubis had been depicted as god of the dead, and a god called Ptah-Seker was the god of resurrection.

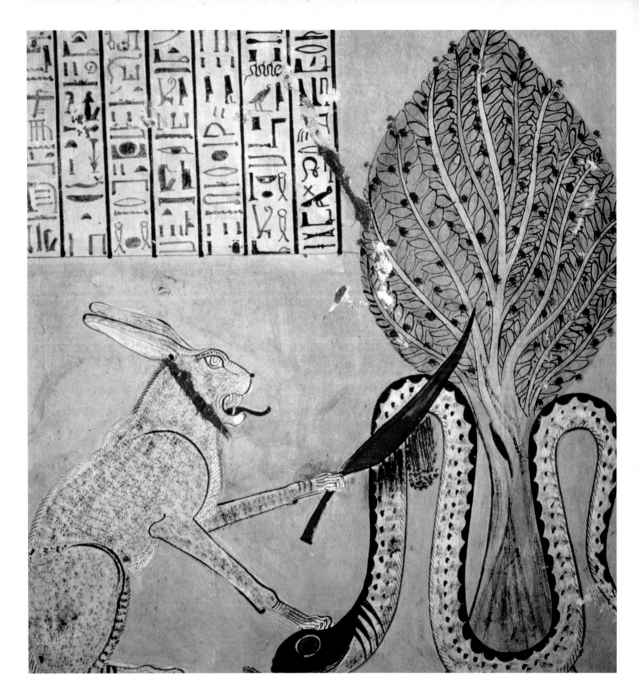

Despite being generally portrayed as a wise pharaoh and a wise and merciful judge, as well as a builder of civilization, Osiris is also suggested in many shorter folk tales to have been snappy, ill-tempered and acid-tongued.

Set

The younger brother of Osiris was trouble from the day he was born, having burst forth from his mother in a sort of DIY Caesarean operation. Set was

In this painting from the era of Rameses IV, Atum-Ra in the form of the Great Cat of Heliopolis kills Apep himself under a sacred tree – yet another version of this myth, sidelining Set. (Everett Collection Historical / Alamy)

one of the first gods to be seen in Egyptian art and myth, being depicted on what is called the Scorpion King mace, a carved stone mace-head dating from pre-Dynastic Egypt. His original centre of worship was at Nubt, near Naqada, in Upper Egypt. (There was also a city called Nubt in Lower Egypt, later renamed Kom Ombo, which was the cult centre for a different god, Sobek.)

Set was thought to be covered with red hair, and people with red hair were said in Ancient Egypt to be favoured by him. In return, such people often chose him as a favourite god. For example, the Ramesside family, the pharaohs Rameses I and II chief among them, were redheads, and they were a dynasty that promoted Set. Perhaps the higher proportion of redheads in the area of Avaris is the reason that place became Lower Egypt's centre of Set's cult in the first place. Or perhaps redheads gravitated there because it was a Set cultural centre.

Set was the god of foreigners, and also the god of the desert. In this latter role he was worshipped by those who wished to be kept safe from the harsh conditions of the desert, and was expected to protect them from sandstorms and help them find water. As god of foreigners, he was both the one to influence them and also the one to defend against them. He also had foreign wives as well as his sister Nephthys. The Semitic and Phoenician goddesses Anat and Astarte were said to be among his consorts.

He was also the master of storms and of warfare, and was popularly worshipped by soldiers and generals. Set is supposed to be the villain of the myth, but things were never that simple.

Horus

The son of Osiris and Isis, Horus represented the living pharaoh, who was considered during his lifetime to be the embodiment of Horus, just as he was considered to become Osiris after death. Horus is actually one of the older gods, having begun as a falcon god (his name derives from the word for falcon) in pre-Dynastic times.

Throughout most of the history of Ancient Egypt, Horus was a sun god like Ra. Sometimes he was considered to be Ra, or blended with him, but he most notably and specifically was associated with the midday sun, because it was from the midday sun that falcons dived upon their prey.

Although Horus was the god of Lower Egypt, the earliest record of his name is in Nekhen in Upper Egypt. Like his rival, Set, Horus was also considered a god of war, and also a god of hunting.

Isis

Isis was the eldest daughter of Geb and Nut, and Queen of Heaven. She appeared as a woman with a model throne for a headdress, but could also transform herself into a bird, and this is reflected in the wings that unfolded from her arms. She was the epitome of wife and mother, and also a goddess of slaves and artists. Most importantly she was a healer by magical means.

As the widow of Osiris, her tears were said to be what caused the Nile to flood. As the mother of Horus, she was by extension the mother of the pharaoh, whoever the pharaoh happened to be. In fact, there are still tribes in sub-Saharan Africa who call a throne the 'mother of the king', which may be a surviving relic of the ancients' view of Isis. Isis was also perhaps the only goddess who was constantly worshipped in all regions of The Two Kingdoms, all the way through its history.

Just because she was a healer, mother, and called upon as protector of the underdog, does not mean Isis did not have a dark side. She was very ambitious, and would stop at nothing to make sure her son got every possible prize and advantage over everyone else.

Thoth

Thoth was the god of wisdom and writing, who also often acted as arbitrator among the gods. He often had the head of a baboon, and sometimes that of an ibis, and was originally the god of the moon. He was a close ally of Osiris, and is often shown assisting him, or even standing in for him, during the judgement of the dead. When judging the dead, he was shown with the ibis head, and when acting as an arbitrator he had the baboon head. He was also the god who disseminated the knowledge of the sciences and the arts of magic.

Thoth was very much a god of diplomacy and balance – his wife was Ma'at, the very personification of order and truth. Whether this attribution came about because his worship was originally based at Khmun, exactly on the borderline between the Two Kingdoms, or whether his temple was based there because of his position as arbitrator, is unknown. In either case, Thoth's impartiality could easily be questioned, due to his alliance with Osiris and his clear delight in trying to embarrass Set.

Nephthys

The younger sister of Isis, Nephthys was the original priestess – her name means 'Lady of the Hall', referring to the temple – and the goddess of lamentation. In this role she, along with her sister, protected the pharaoh for his mummification and journey into the Duat. Nephthys, unlike most of the gods and goddesses, is not usually represented by an animal appearance, although, like Isis, she could turn herself into a bird, usually a kite.

Like Osiris, she appears in the Pyramid Texts from the 5th Dynasty – in the tomb of Unas, from 2345 BC) and spends part of the myth as the nursemaid of Horus, which means she was also considered to be the nursemaid of the

A figurine of Anubis, Osiris's predecessor, then assistant, in judging the dead. (Author's Collection)

13

pharaoh. She also had at least one son of her own, the previous god of the dead, Anubis.

Nephthys is generally considered to be the wife and consort of Set.

Anubis

The jackal-headed god Anubis was the original god of mummification before Osiris. He was the guardian of tombs and protector of the dead, and, rather oddly, he pre-dates both his uncle Osiris and his mother – Nephthys – who both entered the mythology around the 5th Dynasty (2494-2345 BC).

THE DUAT

The Duat is the underworld of Egyptian mythology. It is not quite an underworld in the Greek, Roman, or even Christian sense as a domain of the dead, however. It was more than that, being also the home of the gods and demons, and the world across which the sun travelled at night.

When the early Egyptians looked up at the sky during the day, they saw the sun rise in the east, travel across, and sink into the west. At night they saw the Milky Way, and thought it was a river like the Nile, so they viewed the sun as being the sun god Ra, sailing on that river in a boat.

They also worked out very quickly that Ra's boat travelled back the other way at night, and so deduced that the Milky Way was one half of the river, and that the other half ran underneath the world. This underground half they named the Duat.

They then populated that underworld with dangers and threats, with the gods, and, eventually, with the dead. The Duat was thought to be a real and physical place, with all the geological and geographical features that people saw in the surface world. There was a central river, just like both the Nile and the Milky Way, and there were mountains, islands, deserts, gardens, and buildings. The Duat was also surrounded by the eternal sea of chaos that had existed before the world began, but this sea was much closer to the Duat than its equivalent, the form of the night sky, was to the mortal world.

Unlike many other underworlds in mythology, the Duat's relationship to the dead was not simply as the afterlife or their abode. Rather, it was a realm through which the souls of the dead would have to travel in their attempts to reach the true afterlife, which was called the Field of Offerings. The trials of Ra each night and the mortal life after death were somewhat different, but related. In both cases, the Duat was divided into twelve sections. In Ra's case, he had to switch boats twice to cross it, and be at risk of attack from the giant chaos serpent Apep. Apep lived in the Duat, and it was said that when he thrashed his dragon-like coils, the earth above quaked. A mortal soul would follow the path of this journey and have his life judged by the gods, with his heart weighed against a feather to see how sinful he had been. If the deceased's heart weighed the same as or less than the feather, he was allowed on to Ra's boat to go to the Field of Offerings. If, however, the heart weighed more than the feather, then it was fed to the demon Ammit – part lion, part crocodile, and part hippopotamus. In this way the person's souls – the Egyptians believed everyone had two souls, called the Ba and the Ka – would be destroyed, and so he or she could never go to the paradise of the Field of Offerings. The dead were also at risk of attack from Apep, so it was wise to be prepared, in order that the journey through the Duat was smooth and swift. To prepare the deceased, many of the Egyptian funerary texts were intended as spells or instructions, both warning the deceased of the trials, and advising on the correct responses to them. In particular, a text called the *Amduat* gives a map, as well as details of each of the tests one would face.

Anubis, like his official father, Set, was drawn from the mythology of Upper Egypt, and he also had important duties in the Duat. There, he would preside over the weighing of the heart ceremony, which would decide whether the deceased was too sinful to enter the afterlife.

Wadjet

Protector of Lower Egypt, Wadjet was a goddess in the form of a cobra, who looked after the lands of the Nile Delta. She was the Lady of Flame, able to spit venom at the faces of enemies attacking Ra's boat, just as spitting cobras do. As the protector of Lower Egypt, she was the ideal goddess to protect the baby Horus when necessary. Interestingly, her annual celebration day was on what is now 25th December, now Christmas Day.

All of these various gods, along with many other supernatural beings, had their home in the Duat.

THE JEALOUS BROTHER

Before He was Bad

For a long time, Set was content with his position as the god of Upper Egypt, sharing the duties of protecting The Two Lands with his brother Osiris. Set guided the sandstorms, and helped Egypt by placating foreign forces, or getting them lost in the desert when they were hostile. He and Nephthys had raised their son, Anubis, to be fair in his judgements of the dead, and a stalwart protector of the ancestors and their tombs. Set had other wives, of course, but none of them bore him sons or daughters.

Set also had another important job, as protector of Ra. The brothers' great-grandfather, Ra, who had once called himself Atum, carried the sun across the sky each day, first on his golden barque *Mandjet*, the 'Boat of a Million Years', and then in the afternoon and evening he would switch to the multicoloured 'Evening Boat', *Mesektet*, which was studded with amethysts, emeralds and turquoises. At sunset, Ra descended aboard *Mesektet* through the Western Gates, and into the Duat. There, he would sail under the earth to be reunited with *Mandjet*, ready to rise in the morning.

Like any other soul who journeyed through the Duat, Ra faced trials and tests. Some of these were the same as the ones that the pharaoh, or anyone else, would undergo, but there were other threats to Ra specifically. On each of these journeys, Ra was vulnerable to attack from the evil god, Apep, who bore the simple title 'Enemy of Ra'.

Apep was a different kind of god, who stood for the exact opposite of everything that Ra and the others represented. Where Ra and the other gods brought light, truth and order, Apep brought darkness and chaos. Where the other gods were human with animal heads, who could transform themselves into other creatures, Apep was never human. He was a huge and powerful serpent, 16 yards in length and with a head made of flint. No one ever worshipped Apep, or prayed to him; rather, they prayed for protection from him, and mortal priests conducted an annual rite of burning an effigy of him, to ward off his evil influence on the world.

Each night, Apep would try to catch and kill Ra. Usually he would try to ambush Ra's boat either just after it entered the Duat or just before leaving it. Apep would twist his coils in the river to stop the boat, and fix Ra with his

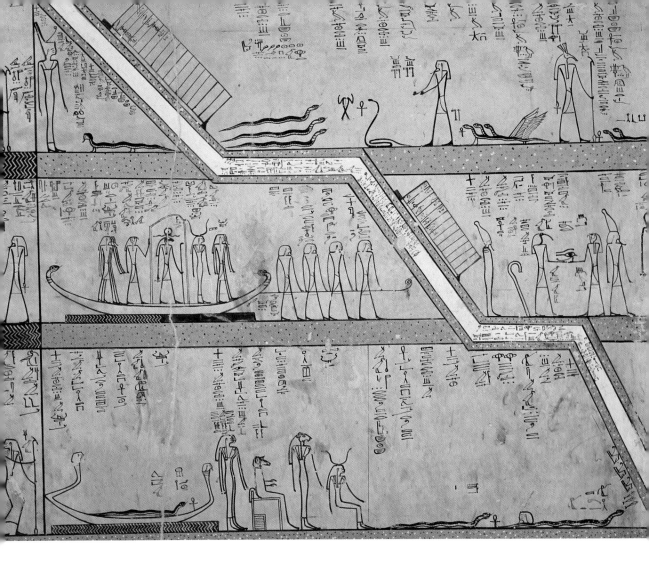

Tomb painting from the tomb of Tuthmose III, around 1425 BC. Note how the style of Egyptian art has changed over time to a much more simplified yet impressionistic style. (The Art Archive / Alamy)

baleful and hypnotic gaze. In this way, Apep hoped to freeze Ra in terror and then devour him.

Fortunately for Ra, he had support. Isis and Nephthys would patrol either riverbank to keep watch for the evil serpent, but Ra's most important ally was none other than his martial great-grandson, Set. Ever-watchful and fiercely loyal, Set took the helm of *Mesektet*, guiding the boat swiftly and surely between the serpent's coils that tried to block the Duat's river. While Ra tried to stave off Apep's hypnotic influence, Set would steer the boat to safety.

Once free of Apep's coils, Set then joined in Ra's fight against the great serpent. As a supernatural being, Apep could only be defeated in specific ways. Set was only too happy first to spit on Apep, and then kick him with his left foot and impale him with a spear. Angered, Apep turned on Set, but this broke his hold on Ra, who was then able to chain him. Finally, Set dispatched Apep with a blade, and Ra burned the body.

Sometimes other gods joined in, and when Ra's daughter Bast, the cat goddess, came on the journey, Set let her deliver the final blow with her claws.

Occasionally, Apep would summon up the courage to attack during the day, and briefly swallow the sun, but Set and the other gods always came to the rescue very quickly, after no more than a few minutes. This battle was repeated each night, since Apep could never be completely killed, as he was a creature who came from the land of the dead and was a part of the eternal primal chaos that surrounded the world. With this assistance to Ra, Set both proved his worth to the world, and made certain that Ra favoured him.

Osiris and Family

While Set was maintaining his reputation and relationship with Ra, his brother Osiris was ruling. In general, Osiris was a wise and benevolent ruler, usually seen as fair by both mortals and the other gods. This was not to say that he was always perfect. He was known for having a sharp sense of humour and a quick temper, which could easily sour relations with the other gods. When stressed, he could be acid-tongued and vindictive. He also had vices.

He had, as gods from most cultures have tended to have, superhuman appetites, and this extended to the wives of other gods. Although he was married to one of his sisters, Isis, he also coveted Set's wife, Nephthys. Indeed, some said that Anubis, supposedly the son of Nephthys and Set, was actually the heir of Osiris, and that Set was as barren as the desert he represented. In either case, when Set discovered his brother's interest in his wife, he was furious.

Set immediately confronted Osiris over this betrayal, demanding that he stay away from Nephthys. Osiris opined that, as the senior of the brothers, it was his right to guide the family's direction, and that, as the junior brother, it was Set's duty to follow his lead. Set, of course, disagreed. As far as he could see, as brothers they were equals, and therefore Osiris should respect his boundaries and wishes, as much as Set respected those of Osiris.

Again and again, Set and Osiris would argue, especially when others whispered about the parentage of Anubis. This argument between them continued for some time, until, inevitably, violence was used. It was not Set who struck the first blow, however: it was Osiris, who began to kick his brother. Osiris was not a warrior like Set, however, and the kicks did no real physical damage. They offended Set, though, increasing the insult he felt from Osiris, and that stung him more than the impact itself. This was the last straw

Cleopatra (the seventh queen with that name, actually), with her son by Julius Caesar, Caesareon, on the southern wall of the temple of Hathor at Dendera. They're showing homage to Hathor, Horus The Elder - who at this period was viewed as the husband of Hathor - and Osiris, who at this point was brother to the Elder Horus. (Library of Congress)

In this tomb painting from circa 1240 BC, Isis has her wings spread, representing Ma'at, or balance, so naturally she'd try to calm her husband down and restore his balance and calm. This image is from the tomb of Rameses the Great's wife Nefertari. (The Print Collector / Alamy)

for Set, who was not the type to take kindly to such an assault. He was, however, the type to bear a grudge. It did not help that Nephthys, annoyed by the darkening mood of both brothers, left Set and went to stay with her sister, so that neither of them would be distracted from their own duties to Ra.

Isis convinced Osiris that it would be wiser to let everyone's tempers cool by taking his wisdom around the whole of the known world. Osiris agreed, and left to tour the world, leaving Isis in charge of Lower Egypt. Isis also looked after her sister, and both were relieved that their husbands would have a chance to calm down. A fuming Set returned to the desert to think about how best to deal with his brother's betrayal. He could not help feeling that perhaps Nephthys had gone to Osiris after all.

Set, like Osiris, had allies – his great-grandfather, Ra, viewed Set as someone who got things done, while 72 other lesser gods viewed him as a preferable leader to Osiris. However, his most immediate ally was the queen of Ethiopia, who ruled Egypt's most powerful neighbour. This was in the days before the Ethiopian queens of Meröe were known to the Egyptians by the name Kandace, and this queen's name was Aso. As the god of foreigners, it was Set's duty to be a sort of ambassador, making sure that Egypt's allies were looked after, and so he had made many foreign friends himself. Aso was both beautiful and a powerful warrior, two traits which Set admired, and therefore she was his closest ally.

Set could not stop thinking about the way his elder brother had treated him, and he began to come to a dark conclusion: if already having all the power was not enough for Osiris, why should being a lesser lord be enough for Set? The more people praised Osiris, the more Set despised him. Aso agreed with him and offered her help to set a trap for Osiris. Set knew his

brother extremely well and gave Aso his exact measurements. Her people were master craftsmen and able to construct a chest to these measurements. It was a magnificent piece of work. Carved from Lebanese cedarwood and ebony from Punt, it was plated with gold and inlaid with ivory. It was so lavish and beautiful that Set knew no one, man or god, could fail to desire it.

When Osiris returned from his travels, Set had already seen that the kingdom could get along perfectly well without him, and so was ready to put his revenge plan into action. Set announced that he would hold a feast, to which all the gods were invited, including his brother. Pretending to have forgotten and forgiven the kick that Osiris gave him, Set played the perfect host to his brother and his brother's wife. He even knelt before Osiris, praising his wisdom. When everyone was suitably relaxed from enjoying the food, beer and wine, and finest dancing girls, Set had some of his 72 friends bring in the fabulous golden chest. As all the gods gasped at its wonder, Set announced a contest: whoever could fit him or herself inside the chest could keep it.

This was an irresistible prize, and everyone in the room rushed forward to try it out. Even Set's 72 friends tried to fit in, to disguise the fact that they knew what was going to happen. Guest after guest tried to squeeze themselves into the chest, shuffling and twisting to try to allow the lid to close, and many of them almost made it. Many times, there was only a finger or toe that did not quite let the lid close, and that was enough to mean that guest did not win. Eventually, of course, Osiris took his turn. He climbed into the chest, and lay down. To his delight, it fitted him snugly, as if it was a second skin. As the lid swung shut on him, Osiris belatedly realized that this was no mere chest – it was a sarcophagus, a coffin! It was already too late to escape, as Set slammed the lid closed. While many of his 72 allies milled around so that the

Judgement of the dead, from the *Book of the Dead*. Left to right, Anubis brings in a soul, the heart is weighed (with the strange-looking Ammit waiting to eat it if it's found wanting) while Thoth records the result. Another soul is being presented by Horus to Osiris, who is flanked by Isis and Nephthys. (The Art Gallery Collection / Alamy)

other guests couldn't see what was really happening, Set and Queen Aso sealed the lid closed with molten lead.

Osiris shouted furiously for them to let him out, and the sarcophagus shook as he wriggled around inside, trying to push the lid off. Set's allies ignored his pleas, and swiftly carried the sarcophagus away into the night. The lead had cooled by now, however, leaving the sarcophagus completely airtight, and, as they ran through the night, it shook less and less, and Osiris's shouts grew fainter. Soon, the air inside had run out, and it was clear that Osiris was dead.

Set and the queen of Ethiopia did not want anyone to know what had really happened to Osiris and decided to dispose of the body so that it could not be found. They took the sarcophagus to the Nile and threw it into the deepest part of the river, where the current was fast enough to carry it far away into the depths of the sea.

Satisfied that Osiris would never be seen again, Set prepared to look after the whole of Egypt while his brother was 'away'.

The Birth of Horus

Isis was most upset at the disappearance of her husband, and although she could not know that Set was responsible, she was suspicious of her brother-in-law. Atum-Ra, the creator and king of the gods, was only concerned with the

(Opposite) *Osiris beguiled into the Chest* by Evelyn Paul.

Soon after Osiris's resurrection with green skin, Little Horus was born. (Ivy Close Images / Alamy)

Horus and Hathor from the Temple at Philae. (Library of Congress)

(Opposite) Horus, the son of Osiris and Isis, was the god of the more fertile and hospitable half of the country, Lower Egypt, which included the lush Nile Delta.

practicalities of the world and was happy enough to leave Set in charge of both halves of the realm. Isis was determined to find her husband, and she set off in search of him, flying in the form of a sparrow. Amazingly, the sarcophagus had not been carried out to sink in the depths of the sea. Instead, it had floated out of the Nile Delta and along the coast to the city of Byblos, in what is now Lebanon. There it had been caught in the roots of a tamarisk tree that grew out of the riverbank.

Over time the tree grew taller, lifting the sarcophagus out of the river. Eventually it was noticed by the people of the city, who reported it to their

The entrance to Horus's temple at Edfu – note the scale of the Horus falcon compared to a human. (Library of Congress)

(Opposite) The vast interior of the Temple of Horus at Edfu, which clearly has plenty of room for gods and men to battle within. (Library of Congress)

king and queen. When King Malcander of Byblos came to see this fantastic gilded chest, he was certain that it was a gift from the gods, to show their approval of his people. He therefore had the whole tree, with the sarcophagus still held in its roots, transplanted to the central courtyard of his palace. There, it would be a grand centrepiece, showing the gods' approval.

Isis had flown over much of the world and found no sign of her husband. She kept searching and eventually reached the land of Byblos, where she soon heard some children talking about this 'gift of the gods'. She recognized the description of the gift at once as the chest into which Osiris had been sealed. She went immediately to the centre of the city of Byblos, where she posed as a healer by anointing some of the maids of the queen of Byblos with oils.

When Queen Astarte heard of this, she asked Isis to help cure her son of a sickness. Isis agreed, in return for the sarcophagus.

The queen, sadly, did not understand who Isis really was and spied on her. When she saw Isis put her son in a fire and fly round him in the form of a sparrow, she burst in to interrupt. Isis resumed her true form and revealed that the young prince was unharmed by the fire. In fact, repetition of the ritual would have made him immortal, but the queen's interruption prevented this, so he was merely cured of his sickness. Nevertheless, Malcander and Astarte of Byblos fulfilled their side of the bargain: since Isis had cured their son, they gave her the sarcophagus. Afterwards, knowing that the tamarisk tree had indeed held a god, they worshipped it even more reverently.

Isis had the sarcophagus loaded onto a boat and sailed back to Egypt. When she reached the Nile Delta, she hid the boat among the reeds and opened the sarcophagus. Osiris, inside, was dead and discoloured, but Isis was not ready to lose her husband yet. She went to her father, Geb, who gave her a spell for resurrecting the dead. The wise Thoth also helped, instructing her on how to preserve Osiris by mummifying him.

Isis applied the sacred oils and potions, wrapped Osiris in linen, and performed the spell that returned him to life. Reunited once more, Osiris and Isis were more concerned for each other than about Set's actions. Osiris, in particular, refused to believe that his brother had done this deliberately. They reassured each other and made love. Before long, Isis gave birth to a son, Horus.

Set the Zombie Slayer

Osiris had been careful to keep a low profile, so that his brother would not know that he had returned until it was too late, and Osiris could expose his treachery to all. Therefore, while Isis tended to their son, who had been stung by a scorpion, Osiris remained on board the boat that had brought him back to Egypt.

The presence of Horus could not go unnoticed for long, however, and since Set's wife Nephthys was helping to raise him, it was not long before Set learned from her that Osiris had returned from the dead. Set and the queen of Ethiopia, therefore, made contact with their 72 co-conspirators to tell them the news. Set did not know where Osiris was, but they all knew that the sooner he was found and destroyed permanently, the less chance there would be of him exposing their crime.

Set and his allies scoured the whole of Egypt for Osiris, all the way from the borders of Ethiopia to the Nile Delta, and west through Libya and the great desert, but without success. Ironically, success finally came when Set stopped looking for Osiris and set off to hunt some wild boar. He had been tracking a pair of boar for some time, when they managed to lose him by hiding in a riverbank thick with reeds. While trying to rediscover their trail

(Opposite) Can a god be killed? Set and his ally Aso, the queen of Ethiopia, were determined to find out what it would take to get rid of Osiris permanently.

29

GODS AND PHARAOHS

It has been quite common for royalty in many cultures to be deified in some way. Usually kings were considered to be either appointed by the culture's gods or to become a god themselves, by ritual or after death.

Ancient Egypt went a lot further with its linking of god and pharaoh. Throughout Egyptian history, the pharaoh was always viewed as a divine being who was essentially an avatar of a god – usually Ra. When the pharaoh died, he would then literally become Osiris. Likewise, Osiris was always the pharaoh, and was depicted with the accoutrements of Egyptian kingship: crook, flail, and crown.

Throughout the reign of a pharaoh, the royal court would also re-enact the important events from mythology at regular intervals, during which the pharaoh would not only take on the role of the most important god – generally Osiris, Ra, or Horus, depending on the myth being re-enacted – but would be considered actually to be the god at that point. It was, perhaps, similar to the way voodoo dancers are considered to be possessed by their gods when they dance. The murder and resurrection of Osiris, for example, was re-enacted around 13th November each year, while the contendings of Set and Horus were re-enacted in the Heb-Sed festival when a pharaoh's reign reached its 30th year. Egyptian mythology is far from unique in having gods and historical mortals interact; Greek mythology is also full of such mixing, with various kings and heroes said be the offspring of gods. However, Egypt got there first. By the time Greek mythology was being written, Greek dynasties were already familiar with Egyptian myth, and the pattern of gods and real people mixing followed naturally from one to the other. There may well be a more practical reason for this mix, however. Egypt's history is so long that, even by the Middle Kingdom in 2000 BC, the Egyptian empire was over a thousand years old, and the early dynasties were considered ancient by the Egyptians themselves. The kings and heroes of the pre-Dynastic era and the Old Kingdom had largely been forgotten, but the continuity of how things were done had to remain stable. The best way to remember things, culturally, has always been in the form of myth and story. It would be very surprising if at least some of the events in the myths were not genuinely based on events in Egypt's history centuries before, since we know that a number of subsequent situations were mythologized even later in Egypt's history, especially by the Graeco-Roman writers, and particularly involving the rivalry of Set and Horus.

among the reeds, Set noticed a glint out of the corner of his eye. It was the gilded surface of the sarcophagus, sitting in a boat camouflaged with reeds. Set was thrilled by his discovery and considered how best to make use of the knowledge. He had immediately forgotten all about the boars, as he had more important prey now.

Set summoned Aso and his other allies and established that Osiris was in a temple on the riverbank, near to which the boat with his sarcophagus was moored. While most of the conspirators spread out to watch for either Isis approaching or Osiris leaving, Set and Aso entered the temple.

Osiris was there and at first assumed Set had come to apologize for accidentally trapping him in the sarcophagus. Set corrected him at once, explaining how he deserved Osiris's throne and had set out to take it. Osiris immediately reached for a weapon to defend himself against the brother who had already killed him once. He was a good fighter, but he was both outnumbered and weakened by his first death. Nevertheless, he put up a good fight against both his brother and the ambitious queen. Swords clashed, the sounds echoing throughout the temple, and the queen of Ethiopia might have lost her life to even the weakened god, if she had not been allied to Set. In the end, though, the outcome was inevitable – Set cut down his brother.

The queen of Ethiopia could not believe what they had done. Osiris had not stayed dead before, after all, and so she was sure it was impossible to destroy a god. Set was determined to prove Aso wrong. As Osiris lay on the temple floor, he hacked the body into more than a dozen pieces, and announced with a laugh that he had done what she thought impossible. When the deed was done, they gathered up the pieces and divided them among their followers, so that each piece could be disposed of separately. Some were thrown into the Nile, others into lakes or deep pits, and still others into the merciless heat of the western desert.

THE VENGEFUL NEPHEW

The First Mummy

As mentioned earlier, Horus had been stung by a scorpion, and Isis had gone to care for him. The young god was soon sufficiently recovered, and so Isis returned to where she had left Osiris and found him missing. Concerned about his safety, she went to her sister, Nephthys, to see if he had gone to visit her. Nephthys said she had not seen him either. Together with Nephthys's son Anubis, and seven scorpions as bodyguards, they went in search of Osiris.

Returning to the temple near his boat, they found plenty of signs of violence – overturned tables, broken chairs and toppled lamps – and, most worryingly of all, bloodstains all over the floor. It was clear to all of them what had happened, and Isis and Nephthys were both equally certain who was responsible. If Osiris had succeeded in fighting off an attack, he would have still been there, triumphant. Since he was not there, and there was so much blood, they knew he had not won the battle that had been fought.

Together, the two goddesses performed the funeral rites for Osiris *in absentia*, and then Isis insisted that Nephthys returned to protect Horus from anything Set might do to the innocent youngster. Though Nephthys did not believe her husband would harm an innocent child, she could not refuse her widowed sister anything. The goddesses, therefore, took Horus to the island of the cobra goddess, Wadjet, and then Isis used her magic to make the island float and move around the kingdom so that Set – or anyone else who might wish harm to the son of Osiris – would never know where to look for it. Isis then constructed a smaller boat for herself out of reeds, and set off to search for the pieces of her husband. It was a long search, taking Isis the length and breadth of Egypt. Sometimes a person would be able to tell her that they had seen something being thrown into the river, and it would turn out of be a piece of the body. At other times she used spells to find them, and when all else failed, she transformed into a bird to spy out the locations from above. Over time, she collected many pieces in her little boat.

Isis was, however, suspicious that some of Set's allies might be spying on her to see if she might resurrect Osiris once more. So, just to be on the safe side, every time she found a piece of the body, she built a shrine and performed the funeral rites on that spot. That way, she hoped, Set and his friends would look in one of those places for Osiris – if they looked at all – while she actually kept all the pieces in her reed boat. Once she had all the pieces, she sailed her boat to the gates of the Duat.

More accurately, once she had all the pieces she could get. It was said that one piece was never found, having been eaten by a catfish; and that it was just as well she had already had a child by him.

Isis then sewed all the pieces together into one body, with many new layers of wrappings. Into the wrappings she sewed protective amulets such as jewellery and stone scarabs, and also parchments with spells of both protection and guidance. Then she performed the resurrection rituals, opening his mouth so he could breathe once more. Once again, Osiris rose, but this time it was only to be parted from his wife. His body having been destroyed, Osiris could no longer live in the mortal world, but would instead rule the Duat as judge of the dead.

Osiris would make the journey that all pharaohs after him had to make through the trials and tests of the Duat, and then would remain there as king

Set and Horus 'celebrate' the union of Upper and Lower Egypt by tying lotus and papyrus reeds to the Pillar of Unity, in a tomb from the 12th Dynasty, circa 1900 BC. (The Art Archive / Alamy)

of the dead, to make sure that all those who followed him would be treated fairly as they undertook their trials. Isis understood this, and, being a goddess, knew she could still visit him there at any time. Osiris had only one request of her in the living world: to make sure that Horus knew what Set had done and to act appropriately.

Isis promised that this would be so.

THE MUMMY

In the Egyptian religion, to reach the Field of Offerings the deceased not only had to pass the various tests in the Duat, but his body needed to be intact and in good condition. It had to be protected for eternity, and the Egyptians decided that the best way to achieve this was to mummify the body.

In purely physical terms, a mummy is a corpse – of a person or animal – that has been preserved by being dried out. There are different types of mummies from ancient cultures around the world, including Egypt and the Incas of Peru. Egyptian mummies are the most famous, not least because Ancient Egypt's mummies were a central element of that civilization's culture and society. The mummy in Ancient Egypt is tied directly to the myth of Osiris and his killing by Set. Essentially, Osiris in the myth becomes the first pharaonic mummy.

The pharaoh in Egypt was always equated directly with various gods, and when he died he was believed to have become Osiris. Mummies in Egypt, as in Peru and elsewhere, were originally formed naturally, when a body was left in the desert with the correct conditions for it to dry out. The earliest surviving Egyptian mummy, British Museum Mummy 32751 (which was originally nicknamed 'Ginger' for its hair colour) was a man who was mummified by natural means, drying out in the desert. No one is quite sure whether he was placed there to be mummified intentionally, or whether he was simply found that way by the Egyptians and then considered to have received some kind of special favour from the gods. He dates from around 3400 BC, almost a thousand years before the earliest recording of the Osiris myth, which means he or someone like him may even have inspired this element of Egyptian beliefs and

funerary rites. In any case, the Egyptians soon got into the habit of mummifying their most important people.

What exactly did the Egyptians do first to their Pharaohs, and, later, to anyone else who wanted eternal life in the hereafter? First of all, the mortuary priests would wash the body in wine. They would then remove the stomach, liver, intestines and lungs. These would be packed in natron – a naturally-occurring salt – to draw out the moisture from them. The heart was left in the body, because the Egyptians believed it was both the seat of the souls (there were two) and of intelligence. They thought the brain was merely the source of nasal mucus – snot, if you will – and so had a special hooked tool to pull it out through the nose. The cadaver was then stuffed with rags and natron, and covered with natron, to absorb all its moisture. Then they left it for 40 days.

Forty days later, the natron and rags were removed and the body washed again, then oiled, to keep the dried-out skin elastic and lifelike. It had to be usable for eternity, after all. Between the Old Kingdom and the Saïte period, from back in 2600 BC until the Persian conquest of 525 BC, the internal organs that had been removed would be placed into canopic jars. These were pottery jars each topped with the head of one of the sons of Horus, each representing one of the compass points. The stomach went into the jar with the jackal head of Duamutef, god of the east. The lungs went into the jar with the baboon-head of Hapi, god of the north. The liver went into the human-headed jar of Imsety, god of the south, while the intestines went into the falcon-headed jar of Qebehsenuef, god of the west. After 525 BC, through to around 30 BC, the desiccated organs were wrapped in linen and put back into the body.

Canopic jars, with lids representing (from left to right): Qebehsenuef, the god of the west; Hapi, god of the north; Duamutef, god of the east; Imseti, god of the south. (Ancient Art & Architecture Collection Ltd / Alamy)

Canopic jars were still buried with the deceased but were just symbolic in the later era.

Any cavities in the body were then stuffed with sawdust, dried leaves, and anything else handy that would pad it out to the shape and size it had been in life. It was then anointed with perfumed oils, after which came the mummy's most distinctive feature: the wrappings. Almost everything was wrapped individually in linen strips: the head, fingers, toes, arms and legs – in that order – and then, finally, the torso. There were multiple layers of linen, with charms and amulets between them. These items, in the form of jewellery and spells on papyrus, were meant to protect and assist the deceased in the Duat, as were the spells recited by an attending priest during the wrapping. The legs were tied together, and, finally, so were the hands, holding a scroll from the *Book of the Dead*, the indispensable guide to making it through the Duat. Mortals were also at risk of attack from Apep just as Ra was, so it was wise to be prepared. In particular,

the *Amduat* gives a map, as well as details of each of the tests.

In many ways, Set's protection of Ra during his journey through the Duat is echoed by the embalmers and relatives of the deceased, who helped a deceased person – whether a pharaoh or otherwise – on their journey after death. By ensuring that the deceased had the right amulets and spells, that the *Amduat* would guide them, and that they would thus be able to avoid Apep on the way to the heart-weighing, they were, in a way, performing the role that Set played each night. Perhaps this is another reason why he remained such a memorable god, who still had worshippers and a cult even when demonized as a villain: everyone who helped bury a loved one did something good that Set did.

With the texts safely added, the whole package was then bound in wider lined strips, glued down with plant resin, and the outer surface painted as a portrait of Osiris. Once wrapped in rougher cloth, the mummy was ready.

(Previous page) When Set and Horus finally came to outright battle, they both had allies, as mortal armies supported their chosen gods.

A real solar barque, reconstructed from a buried boat at Giza. Ra's boat *Mandjet* would be like this, as would the boats constructed by Set and Horus for their race. (Photograph by Berthold Werner)

Horus vs Set

As a child, Horus had been raised on Wadjet's moving island, while Set watched over both of the Two Kingdoms, making himself appear to be fulfilling a reluctant duty in taking care of his late brother's land during his absence, as well as still ruling his own half. Eventually, however, the time came when Horus was ready to seek his father's place. Isis fulfilled her promise to her husband by telling Horus what had happened to his father. As he learned the story, Horus grew more and more angry at what his uncle had done.

Osiris then visited the living world for one day, to judge his son's readiness for the task of seeking justice. He asked his son, 'What is the noblest thing a man can do?' Horus replied, 'Avenge the evil done to his father and mother.' Osiris then asked, 'What is the best animal for seeking revenge?' Horus said that would be a horse. For a moment, Osiris was puzzled, as this was not the sort of answer he had expected. He asked Horus why he did not choose a lion instead. Horus said simply, 'A lion is best for a man in need of help of teeth and claws to defend himself with, but a horse is best for pursuing a fleeing enemy and cutting off his escape.'

Osiris saw immediately that this was indeed the right answer, and that Horus was not just giving in to anger but was thinking about his actions and his strategy. With those words, Horus had proved his wisdom to Osiris, and Osiris could return to the Duat confident that his son was ready to make things right.

Escorted by his mother, Horus left Wadjet's island at Chemmis and travelled to Heliopolis, to present himself to the grand council of the gods, presided over by the creator and king of the gods, Ra. There, Horus revealed what Set had done to Osiris and claimed that Osiris's throne – and vengeance upon Set – was his birthright.

The gods were not quite sure what to make of this. Most of them knew what had happened between Set and Osiris, and while many disapproved of Set's actions, all of them agreed that they could not simply hand Egypt over to an untested child; this was a job that required specialist education and lots of experience. Ra, in particular, was in favour of Set. He felt that Set was an experienced ruler who had proven his worth, and he also valued his contribution and loyalty as the protector of Ra on his journey each night. Shu, the god of the winds, and Thoth, the

god of wisdom, sided with Horus and Isis, feeling that this would be more just. Thinking that the matter was settled, Isis asked Shu to tell Osiris of the result, which he did. Ra was angered by this, since, as king of the gods, he felt he should have the final say.

The triumphant and imposing pylons, as archaeologists call them, of the Temple of Horus at Edfu. (Library of Congress)

Set suggested a simpler way to decide the matter: a trial by combat. Horus was free to step outside with Set and fight him for the throne. Horus agreed eagerly and took on Set in single combat. Although Horus was younger and faster, Set was far more experienced at warfare, and the fight quickly turned against the younger god. Before Set could defeat him, however, the other gods emerged from their council chamber, and Thoth separated the combatants. This, the god of wisdom insisted, was not the way they should decide such matters.

Time passed differently for gods than for mortals, and by the time Ra looked upon Set and Horus in the council chamber once more, 80 years had passed, and Set's main ally, Queen Aso, had died. Now Set had fewer allies, with even his mother, Nut, saying Horus should be given the throne. Ra would still have preferred the stronger and more experienced Set and thought that Horus was a weakling who could not hold the throne, but he knew he must be fair and even-handed and hear both cases.

Set pointed out that he had ruled in his brother's stead for years, and that everyone knew he was the loyal one who defended Ra from Apep every day. Without him, he said, Ra would have been destroyed long ago, and the world lost to chaos. Many of the gods appreciated this point and agreed that Set, as the elder candidate, was a more suitable ruler. Thoth disagreed, however, and said that it could not be right to give the throne to a brother when the rightful heir is able to sit upon it.

During a break in deliberations, Isis disguised herself as a beautiful widow, and made sure that Set noticed her. She told Set in front of the other gods that she was the widow of a farmer, who, with her son, was to be evicted from their farm and have their cattle confiscated. Set was enraged at such an injustice, and promised to exact punishment for such a crime. Isis immediately revealed her true identity and pointed out to the assembled gods that Set had condemned himself by admitting that his own claim was by his own standards unjust.

The gods immediately thought to give the throne to Horus, but Ra, still willing to believe the best of Set, allowed Set to challenge Horus to a less lethal form of contest than single combat. The first challenge was for both of them to transform into hippopotami and see who could stay underwater the longest. This they did, but after three months, Isis grew suspicious that Set, who was associated with this animal, had an unfair advantage and had done something to her son. She, therefore, made a harpoon, and threw it into the water where she could see a hippo which she believed to be Set. Unfortunately, Horus had been holding his own in the contest, and had not been harmed by Set, and this was the hippo that she hit. Horus thrashed in pain, coming to the surface immediately.

Aerial view of the Temple of Horus. (Library of Congress)

Horrified by her error, Isis healed her son, and then threw the harpoon at the correct hippo, whom she knew would now seem to have won the contest by staying underwater longer. Pierced by the copper spear, Set erupted from the water in anger and agony, to find Isis waiting to finish him off. Set pleaded with her to see what she had done, and to think about how she was about to commit the same crime for which she condemned him - fratricide. At this reminder, Isis stepped back, much to the annoyance of her son, who saw this as a missed opportunity for a just revenge.

Horus was so incensed, in fact, that he struck off his mother's head in a tantrum, but she was a goddess and so this merely turned her into a statue for a while, until he placed her head back upon her body. Angered in turn by his disrespectful behaviour, Set put out Horus's eye as a punishment. Lashing out in pain, Horus in turn castrated Set.

By now the other gods had noticed what was happening. Hathor healed the wounded combatants, and Ra summoned them to appear before him again. Angry at the escalation of their conflict to include Isis, Ra commanded them to make peace. Set agreed to the request of his grandfather, and invited Horus to his home for a feast. This was a pretence, however, so that Set could trick Horus into eating Set's semen, hidden in the food, and thus embarrass the younger god by having sexually dominated him. If his plan succeeded, Horus would be a laughing stock, and the gods would award Set the throne.

Isis, however, had already been suspicious, and helped her son to turn the tables on Set, who himself consumed the semen, which Isis had switched from Horus's plate onto some lettuce on Set's plate. When Isis then revealed this to the rest of the gods, Set was mocked and laughed at, and Thoth declared that

Bas-relief in the heart of the temple in Edfu, Egypt depicting Horus and his family. (Library of Congress)

if this was considered a challenge, then Horus had won. However, because Isis had interfered, Set's humiliation did not mean that it was a victory for Horus, as he himself had not actually been the one to trick Set.

The next challenge for the pair was simple: they were each to build a boat of stone and hold a race. Set played fairly by the rules, building a boat made

(Opposite) *Horus and Set* by Evelyn Paul.

ANIMALS AND GODS

One of the most distinctive things about artworks depicting the Egyptian gods – whether tomb paintings or statues – is that most of them were depicted at least partially in an animal form. Specifically, they were usually shown as a human figure with the head of a bird or animal. At other times they were shown with a sun or moon, depending on whether they had solar or lunar connections, and often this was on top of a bird or animal head. For example, Horus had the head of a falcon, as did Ra, but because Ra was the embodiment of the sun, he was shown with the sun resting on top of the falcon's head. Horus often had a crown on top of his falcon-head. Some gods were depicted wholly as animals, such as Khepri, who was always shown as a scarab beetle, Wadjet the cobra goddess, and Taweret, the goddess of pregnancy and birth, who was shown as a hippopotamus that stood upright on its hind legs.

The Egyptians did not worship animals, although they farmed them for food and they kept pets. That said, some animals were also kept in cages or enclosures as symbols of a god or goddess, while others simply lived in temples and were considered sacred. These pets and sacred animals were often mummified when they died, like a member of the family.

The Ancient Egyptians saw things in certain animal behaviours that reminded them of attributes of different gods. These similarities that the Egyptians saw between their gods and their animals are not blatantly obvious to modern eyes. Anubis, who is in charge of weighing the hearts of the dead to determine whether they were good or bad, for example, has the head of a jackal. This is because a jackal, as a carrion-eater, can tell good meat from bad in a dead creature. The Ancient Egyptians simply modified this to being able to tell good from bad in the deceased's heart.

Scarab beetles were seen to roll balls of dung along, just like the fiery ball of the sun rolled along the sky, so – even though Ra was also thought to travel in a boat – the beetles became associated with the god Khepri, who was a giant beetle who pushed the sun along. They were also associated with Osiris and Horus as symbols of rebirth, because they would bury themselves in the sands in hard times, and then reappear as if reborn later.

The best-known animal sacred to the Ancient Egyptians was, of course, the cat. Cats had poise and grace, and were effective hunters that protected grain from rodents – just the sort of graceful justice you might expect from Bast, the daughter of Ra. The least-known animal in Egyptian terms, however, was the one that shared its face with Set. Set has an animal head, but the type of animal is unknown. In fact most sources seem to suggest that the Set animal is some kind of hybrid made up of

The most familiar example of Ancient Egypt's linking of animals and gods – the sacred cat, in this case a statue of Bast. (Author's Collection)

such diverse creatures as donkeys and giraffes, probably because the seated animal shown in hieroglyphics to represent Set's name looks like a mixture of these. However, there may in fact be a single answer to the question of the Set animal.

Look at Set's nose and ears, and look at this aardvark. The Set animal in hieroglyphics is shown in the triangular sitting position that a dog or cat sits in, but an aardvark cannot sit that way, which may be why the hieroglyph looks like it's made from different animals. (Life on white / Alamy)

of stone, but Horus instead built his boat out of wood and rushes, which he covered with a thin layer of plaster to look like stone. Of course as soon as the boats were placed in the Nile, Set's boat sank like, well, a stone, while Horus paddled his boat away at high speed. Once in the river, Set immediately transformed into a hippopotamus, and pursued Horus's boat. He surged up from under it, smashing the flimsy wood and rushes into dozens of pieces.

Horus, now enraged, was determined that it was time to kill Set, but the other gods refused to let him. Frustrated, he went to Saïs, to appeal to his grandmother, Nut. He told her how all the judgements so far had pointed to him as deserving the throne, but still it had not been given to him.

Meanwhile, Ra and Osiris had argued about who should take the throne. Ra knew Set as a loyal ally who protected him from Apep, but Osiris had been murdered by him and that coloured his view. Now that he was king of the underworld, Osiris had found that he was in charge of many beings and monsters who had no fear of either gods or mortals, but who had the power to destroy both, if they were wrongdoers. Even the stars themselves could be brought down by them, taken below the western horizon and into the Duat, to be judged by Osiris and either destroyed or sent into the afterlife.

Ra viewed this as a threat, and one which he could not resist. If denying the son and heir his father's throne would lead to the destruction of the heavens and the earth by said vengeful father's crew of underworld creatures, then that son must be given the throne. Ra, therefore, summoned the gods once more and pronounced his final judgement: Horus would be given his father's throne.

Because Ra had been forced into this decision, he was determined to make his own point as creator and king of the gods. He therefore also decreed that Set would not be punished for his actions but would keep the throne of Upper Egypt, and he would continue to accompany Ra on his daily journey, and that his voice would be heard in the thunder. While Horus would sit on his father's throne, it would be as god of Lower Egypt, not of the whole empire.

The Final Conflict

For 363 years, this situation worked, with Horus ruling Lower Egypt in the north, and Set ruling Upper Egypt in the south. Eventually, however, tensions began to mount again, as both gods wanted to rule a unified realm. Horus wanted Set to lose his kingdom as punishment for the murder of Osiris, while Set wanted to recover the half of the kingdom he had originally taken from his brother.

As there was tension between the gods, so too was there tension in the mortal world, as the peoples of each half of the kingdom rallied behind their ruling god and fought the followers of the other. Each god was very protective of his people and viewed the actions of the other's followers as an insult. When Horus began moving an army towards Nubia – and thus in the direction of Upper Egypt – Set took this to be an attack, and had his people rise in open rebellion. If the gods would not curb Horus's vendetta, Set thought, then he would.

Set gathered an army of gods and mortals, and travelled north to meet Horus at Edfu, where Horus was based at his temple. Horus, knowing that the final reckoning was coming, had Thoth turn him into a falcon as bright as the midday sun.

Horus then flew up to the sun, from where he could see the whole of Set's massive army darkening the earth. Set, meanwhile, was looking out for his nephew, but because Horus appeared to be at one with the sun, Set was blinded by the light and could not see him. As the armies met between the riverbank and the temple, Horus dived into the midst of Set's forces. Being as bright as the midday sun in this form, he blinded the warriors who followed Set, and so when they hacked about themselves, trying to fight off the blinding light, they hit each other instead of Horus or his warriors. By the time Set's army reached Horus's army, their numbers had been depleted as they had blindly hacked off each other's limbs and cracked each other's skulls.

Nevertheless, the two armies did meet, and, in the midst of them, so did the two gods. All along the riverbank, gods, demigods, and wizards among Set's followers turned themselves into hippopotami and crocodiles to ambush Horus's followers on the riverside. Set, meanwhile, equipped himself with sword and spear, and launched himself at Horus. Horus had learned much since their last duel, and was able to defend himself far more effectively than before. Nevertheless, the onslaught of Set's blades drove him back towards a nearby pyramid. Set pressed home his attack, certain of victory. He could see that Horus had improved his skills, but knew that his longer experience of battles would win through in the end.

As the pair duelled at the heart of the battle, however, Thoth worked his famed magic, using both spells and his knowledge of the sciences to make the weapons of Horus's army strong enough to pierce even the thickest scales and hide. Set and Horus, meanwhile, continued to cut and thrust at each other

with their own swords and spears, duelling up and down the steps of nearby pyramids before Horus began to push Set back through the temple.

Though the two gods were evenly matched, Thoth's help with Horus's army meant Set's army was in trouble. As it fell back under the onslaught of stronger weapons, Set was soon outnumbered. As Set's followers were brought down by Thoth's strengthened blades, the survivors began to flee south. Horus's army swept on after them, pursuing them deep into Upper Egypt. Recognizing that his followers were defeated, Set broke off and fled the temple of Edfu for the river. While his army pursued the remnants of Set's forces, Horus fought his way through the stragglers and most fanatical followers of Set, to the river. He borrowed a boat from Ra and took to the river in pursuit of Set.

Set had gone north towards Lower Egypt, thinking both to draw Horus away from doing further harm to his army, and to be able to take the throne as soon as he had killed his nephew. Set remembered how he had been able to destroy Horus's fake stone boat before, and planned to lure him into a trap where he could do the same thing again. This time he intended not just to destroy the boat but to kill his nephew.

Unfortunately, Horus had also remembered what happened with the boats before, and this time he was ready for Set's attack. Set dived deep in order to approach Horus unseen, but Horus's healed eye was better than his original, and so Horus was waiting for him when he surfaced. Horus hurled his spear down at Set as Set burst forth from the waters. The spear slammed into the angry god, but it did not stop him. He leapt upwards, almost turning Horus's boat over. Horus struggled to remain standing steady in order to hurl more spears at Set. Set slammed his body against the boat, trying to knock Horus into the jaws of the waiting crocodiles, but Horus jumped out at the last second and straddled both banks of the river like a colossus. From there, Horus stabbed downwards, impaling Set upon a harpoon. Set struggled to free himself, but too late. Horus drew his sword and decapitated his nemesis with a single stroke.

Mere decapitation was not enough to permanently destroy a god, of course, but it was more than enough to be a decisive defeat. The severed head disappeared as the rest of the hippo transformed into a beaten and humiliated Set, who had no choice but to kneel before Horus and accept defeat. This was proof enough for all the gods – even Ra – that Horus was indeed capable of ruling a unified Egypt, and so Ra pronounced that henceforth Horus's throne would be that of both Upper and Lower Egypt together. Set returned to his duties as Ra's bodyguard and protector against the desert, while Horus ruled wisely with the advice of Isis and Thoth. Justice was finally done.

(Opposite) Has Set made a tactical error by repeating an earlier trick? In either case, the final showdown reflected the fact that hippopotami, not crocodiles, were considered the most dangerous animals in the Nile.

TO THE VICTOR THE SPOILS

It may seem strange that two opponents with such a violent rivalry, engaged in a civil war, should be happy to engage in such non-lethal challenges as staying underwater, and a boat race. However, such challenging – and generally non-fatal – sports were no strangers in Ancient Egypt.

Perhaps understandably, as with the development of so many sports in other societies throughout history, most Ancient Egyptian sports originated with a martial element, as practice or training for warfare. Many martial skills are known to have been played as sports because they were displayed in tomb paintings. Archery, for example, was a popular contest, in which, as today, archers would shoot at flat target boards, on each of which was hung a brass ring. The competing archers would try to place as many arrows into the board through the ring as they could.

Fencing was practiced with special hardened sticks not unlike modern police batons, which were dual-wielded and could be held along the forearm in order to aid with blocking attacks. In the movie *The Mummy Returns*, the duel between the two lead female characters using anachronistic Japanese sai (which obviously didn't exist in Ancient Egypt) is shot to resemble Egyptian paintings of boys fencing with these sticks.

Other physical sports with obvious military applications included horse-racing, wrestling, boxing, weight-lifting, swimming, javelin-throwing, and so on. They also, however, held competitions for other sports that even schoolchildren would recognize today. For example, they held tug-of-war contests, though in Ancient Egypt they didn't use a rope between the teams – each team member would wrap their arms around the teammate in front, and the front person of each team would grasp their opponent's wrists, and the teams would then try to pull each other over. In fact, Egyptians still do this version of the game today.

The Egyptians also had some surprisingly modern sports, including handball, which is shown in tomb paintings at Saqqara as being a game for four girls, just like modern Beach Volleyball… They even had a game – depicted on tombs at Beni Hassan – that looks just like hockey, and a variation of this that used a hoop instead of a ball. Games aren't always sports, of course. The Egyptians even had a draughts or checkers-like board game (a set was found in Tutenkhamun's tomb) and gambled on dice made from bones.

As for underwater breath-holding and boat racing, well, breath-holding probably comes under swimming. The Egyptians did host boat races, however, with rowers pulling to the call of a helmsman, much like the Oxford vs Cambridge boat race today. Again, this had a clear military training element to it, as galleys – oar-powered warships – were the order of the day back then. At least the mortals who engaged in these sports didn't have to build their own boats out of stone.

HISTORY AND WARFARE

I've Heard it Both Ways

Like all stories, the tale of the enmity between Set and Horus has varied over the millennia and over many retellings. This was inevitable, not simply because stories always change as new people from different societies tell them, but also because the original religious context of the story has largely been lost. That said, some of the political context remains in the fragments of the story that have survived longest.

There are both major and minor variations in the myth, ranging from simply how many pieces Osiris was cut into (usually varying between 12 and 16 – though at least one version gives 42 – with most retellings splitting the difference and calling it 14), or even if he was cut up at all. In some versions, Set and Horus duel alone, while in others they have allies and armies.

There is no surviving complete native Egyptian version of the myth of Set, Horus, and Osiris. Episodes from the overall story are found as far back as the 5th Dynasty, but the earliest complete telling of the myth that survives from classical antiquity is the version told by the Greek writer and Roman citizen, Plutarch, in his *Moralia*, published in AD 100. Like other Greek and Roman historians, Plutarch tells a good story, targeted towards an audience and a world of the first century AD. This means he added things to the story that reflect things that happened long after the myth was originally created. He also imported a number of elements from Greek myth, most notably following Herodotus's lead in equating Set with the Greek figure of Typhon, the 'father of monsters'. In fact, the text of Plutarch's *De Iside et Osiride*

Herodotus, whose linking of Set with Typhon is followed up on by Plutarch. Which is ironic, as Plutarch hated Herodotus and in fact authored a vicious criticism of him, entitled *The Malice of Herodotus*.

The Greeks ruled Egypt for several centuries, with the Ptolemies and Cleopatras being the most famous of their pharaohs. But the most successful Greek conqueror was also pharaoh, and seen here in monumental sculpture form in Pharaonic headdress: Alexander the Great. (The Art Archive / Alamy)

uses the name Typhon in place of Set throughout. Plutarch also has Horus (the Younger) conceived before Osiris dies in the sarcophagus.

The Greek writer Herodotus, who was born about 50 years after Cambyses conquered Egypt, and died in 425 BC, wrote down the tale of the wars between the Greeks and Persians, which included much about the state of Egypt in the previous hundred years, before and after the conquest of Cambyses. This is included in his famous work *Histories.* Herodotus is known for having been slightly gullible in his researches, but remains one of the earliest written sources for a lot of history in the region. Although his treatment of Ancient Egypt and the beliefs of its people in the second book of the *Histories* is somewhat fanciful (he said they use their feet to make bread, due to religious taboos, for example), it's not judgemental.

Some of the post-Herodotus creation myths that do survive from Ptolemaic times, when Egypt was ruled by Greek pharaohs, have Osiris being named Horus the Elder before his death. These versions take the view that because Osiris is the name for the ruler of the underworld, he could only have been called that after he died and went there. In fact, Plutarch's version of the Egyptian creation myth differs from what we know of both original versions in a number of ways. For example, Plutarch describes *five* children of Geb and Nut: Osiris, Horus the Elder, Set, Isis, and Nephthys. This is a problem because it means there would be ten members of the Ennead – a Greek word meaning a group of nine! He also has Set being the elder brother at some points and younger at others.

However, although Plutarch's is the earliest complete version of the Set and Horus story, it is far from being the earliest version of the whole tale, which began to be told in pre-Dynastic times.

The tales of the gods were undoubtedly first told as oral stories, around campfires and in temples. The first written version of the story of Osiris's death and Set and Horus's feud was as part of the Pyramid Texts.

Plutarch was writing 2,500 years after these original fragments, so there is no surprise that chunks of the original tales had been forgotten. Aside from adding contemporary Greek elements, Plutarch also smoothed over some of the gaps with parts of other fragmentary Egyptian stories. For example, at one point in Plutarch's version, Set cuts off Osiris's manhood and throws it into the Nile, where it is eaten by a catfish. This is in fact a borrowing from a totally different Egyptian folk tale, *The Tale of Two Brothers*, which was recorded onto papyrus around 1200 BC. *The Tale of Two Brothers* was perhaps chosen for this borrowing because it features two feuding brothers, just like Set and Horus, although the brothers in this story were not gods. Having said that, *The Tale of Two Brothers* may have itself been inspired by an earlier version of the actual Set and Horus myth. After all, *The Tale of Two Brothers* was written during the reign of Seti II, part of the dynasty that venerated Set and indeed took the throne name (Seti) from him. Oddly enough, one part of the original Ancient

The Pyramid of Djoser at Saqqara. This pyramid is right next door to the original Pyramid of Unas, which has largely crumbled away into a rough hill. It would originally have looked more like this one. (Library of Congress)

Egyptian version that does survive is the ending, and, surprisingly, it ends on a cliffhanger. Instead of Horus being awarded the throne, it was said that the struggle would continue until the chaos of the end of the world, at which point Osiris would return to rule Egypt.

Casting Against Type

In the earlier dynasties, Set had been one of the good gods, who helmed the 'Boat of a Million Years', and defended Ra against the evil serpent Apep, who was the one who wanted to bring darkness and chaos. Then, by the time of the Ptolemies, when Herodotus was writing, Set was firmly established as a cosmic villain. He was the usurper, who wished to bring chaos to the world.

Herodotus identified Set with the Greek 'father of monsters', Typhon, an evil Titan who rebelled against the gods. From that point onwards, writers and folklorists – and even the Egyptian priesthood itself – would cast Set in that role, as the arch-villain of myth. It is doubly ironic that he was equated with Typhon, as that Greek Titan had the coils of a giant serpent, the most obvious trait of the original villain, Apep. By the time of Ptolemaic Egypt, in fact, Set's attributes – as a bringer of chaos and darkness – were all those that had once been the attributes of Apep.

This did not happen by accident. It is no coincidence that the god of foreigners was made into a figure of evil at a time when the kingdom was being ruled by foreigners. The story of Set's changing morals and allegiances is pretty much the chronological story of Egypt's governance.

Back in pre-Dynastic times, Set and Horus were considered the rulers of Upper and Lower Egypt respectively, but both gods were worshipped equally in both kingdoms. In this period, Set was viewed as a kind of a trickster god like the Norse god (and Marvel comics villain) Loki, the Native American spirit Coyote, or the Afro-Caribbean spider god Anansi. These are gods whose attempts to trick people are intended to teach people to think about what they say and do. He is portrayed this way in the New Kingdom story *The Tale Of Truth And Falsehood*, only a fragment of which survives on papyrus dating from around 1250 BC. Here, Set is not really good or evil, but a god who keeps people on their toes.

Throughout the dynasties of Egypt, there was a certain amount of both political and religious struggle between the two kingdoms. This is reflected in the fact that there are two creation myths, and two sets of original gods: the nine gods of the Ennead in Upper Egypt, and the eight gods of the Ogdoad in Lower Egypt. When Upper Egypt was stronger, the Ennead was more popular, and when Lower Egypt was stronger, so the Ogdoad was more likely to be favoured.

Both the Ennead and Ogdoad, however, were only really set in stone around the 5th and 6th dynasties, while Set and Horus – as individual deities – were much older. Horus was first worshipped as a local patron deity in Nekhen, in Upper Egypt, in pre-dynastic times, while Set came along in the 2nd Dynasty. This immediately provided a motive for a rivalry between them, as the cult of Set – and his priesthood – began to take over from the cult of Horus, which had been established for a few centuries already. During this 2nd Dynasty, the *serekh*, or symbol, of King Peribsen's name – which had been surmounted by a Horus falcon in the 1st Dynasty – was surmounted by a Set animal, indicating that there had been a struggle between the priesthoods of the two gods that the cult of Set had now won. Later, the fifth and final Pharaoh of the 2nd Dynasty, Khasekhemwy, surmounted his *serekh* with both the falcon of Horus and a Set animal, showing the two now to be equals.

In other words, Horus was now the god of Lower Egypt, and Set the god of Upper Egypt, both with equal importance to the pharaoh. This continued until the period between 1800 BC to 1560 BC or so, when the

Hyksos began to take over Lower Egypt until eventually they ruled the Nile Delta, from a capital they had set up at Avaris. They chose Set, originally Upper Egypt's chief god, the god of foreigners and the god they found most similar to their own chief god, as their patron, and so Set became worshipped as the chief god over Lower Egypt as well. In fact the Hyksos Pharaoh Apophis insisted that Set should be the only god worshipped at all. This was incomprehensible to the Ancient Egyptians, that one god could usurp the positions of the others.

This was bound to provoke a reaction, and, sure enough, the Egyptians rose up and expelled the Hyksos, installing Ahmose I as pharaoh. The new rulers in Thebes were keen to reverse all the cultural changes imposed by the foreign rulers, and that included Set's position as chief god. That said, Set was still one of Egypt's own pantheon, and so his cult at Avaris remained strong on its home ground, and the garrison of soldiers that Ahmose put there became a new generation of his priesthood. Nevertheless, the xenophobia that Hyksos rule had left in Egyptians meant that Set was now viewed with more suspicion and distaste than before.

That new generation of Set's priesthood at Avaris, however, came to the fore with the founding of the 19th Dynasty, around 1295 BC, by Rameses I. Several of his descendants who followed him as pharaoh were actually named for Set. In particular the pharaohs' name Seti meant 'man of Set', and Setnakht meant 'Set is strong'. Likewise, Rameses II erected the 'Four Hundred Years' Stele at Pi-Ramesses, commemorating the 400th anniversary of Set's priesthood in Lower Egypt.

Later, around the 22nd Dynasty, from 943 to 716 BC, Egypt was ruled by the descendants of Libyans – foreign rulers again – and Set was again identified with overtly darker gods. Some Egyptians compared him to the Hittite god Teshub, because both were storm gods. However Set's reputation was further blackened by royal and priestly propaganda which equated Set with his own ancient enemy, Apep. Apophis, of course, the foreign king who had once put Set above all others, shared the Greek name for Apep. The comparison was therefore perhaps inevitable, and now even some of the carvings of Set on temples were replaced with those of other gods, such as the crocodile god Sobek. Within three hundred years, the Persians were on the march, and Cambyses had taken Egypt – another foreign ruler surely favoured by the god of foreigners.

The really big enemies of the Persians, however, were soon to be the Greeks, and it was the Greek writers Herodotus and Plutarch who gave us the earliest complete surviving versions of the myth. Although they themselves were somewhat foreign, the Greeks could not help but maintain the idea of Set being the evil god, as he was now so associated with Apophis, and no longer remembered as Ra's companion and loyal ally. Set's fate was sealed; he was forever more to be the villain.

Conquest of Cambyses

There were times in Egypt's recorded history that were just as game-changing as the events of myth and legend. More importantly, these times were reflected in the myths and legends, as the tales and their characters changed to reflect the social and political realities of the country. This included the myth of Set and Horus, and the characters and natures of the gods involved – especially Set who was much less evil before the Persians came to Egypt…

Although Egypt maintained an official policy that all the living pharaohs were descended from the same gods, The Two Kingdoms had really undergone several regime changes, and even outright invasions, over the course of time. By 1640 BC, around the time of the 14th Dynasty, the Hyksos people – the word deriving from the Ancient Egyptian for 'rulers of foreign lands' – had become pharaohs through dominance in politics.

In the 8th century BC, Egypt became the target for a less subtle takeover. The Nubian kings to the south had seen that Egypt was becoming weaker and more divided, long past the heights it had achieved in the past. The Nubians first infiltrated Egyptian politics by marrying off their daughters to members of the Egyptian court. When the time was right, and Egypt's politics were sufficiently destabilized, the Nubian King Piye marched north, defeating all of Egypt's leaders. Soon, he was settled at Thebes, and crowned pharaoh. He and his family had founded the 25th Dynasty, but made the rulers he had defeated

Cambyses and Psamtik III confront each other to discuss terms, in an 1841 painting. (filled with anachronistic costumes) by Jean Adrien Guignet (The Art Archive / Alamy)

This 19th century painting shows the Persians of Cambyses hurling cats into Pelusium to put off the cat-worshipping defenders. Thankfully this is a Victorian myth, though the Greek historian Palyaenus claimed that the Persians did carry cats with them in their chariots to discourage Egyptian archers from shooting at them. (North Wind Picture Archives / Alamy)

into regional governors, so that most of the people in towns and cities were still working for the same rulers.

The Nubian pharaohs eventually got into a Cold War with the Assyrians. Regular border conflicts flared up, and Egypt's usual allies had all drifted away, or had their own problems to handle. Egypt had one big disadvantage when compared to the Assyrians: a lack of trees. With more trees to cut down, the Assyrians could turn more logs into charcoal than the Egyptians; with more charcoal, the Assyrians could smelt more iron; and with more iron, they could make more swords, spearheads, and arrowheads. This they did, and then, when the Cold War turned hot, they struck.

An Assyrian army with weapons of iron and steel smashed into Egypt, making for the capital, Thebes. Once there, they looted the city of its treasures, and burned out the temples and palaces of its Nubian rulers. The Assyrians then made a deal with a noble family from the Egyptian city of Saïs, and made them puppet pharaohs.

Now that the Egyptians had Egyptian pharaohs again, tribute would flow smoothly south and east to Assyria, and the Assyrians did not have to bother using people and resources to rule Egypt.

In 525 BC, greedy eyes turned towards Egypt, whose fertile Nile Delta and supplies of gold were very tempting targets for Cambyses II, ruler of the mighty Persian Empire. Cambyses' father, Cyrus the Great, had previously started a campaign against Egypt, but had died in a battle against nomadic archers before his invasion could be launched. Cambyses was determined to fulfil his father's ambition, and so he soon gathered his generals and advisers around him. In the four years since his father had died, his spies had been bringing Cambyses news of everything that happened in Egypt. 'Now', he told his generals, 'the Egyptian government is collapsing. The pharaoh can neither hold on to power, look after his people, nor defend his borders.'

One of these generals was a man named Phanes of Helicarnassus, a Greek mercenary who had once served with the Egyptian army. 'I'm not surprised,' Phanes said. 'I used to work for the Pharaoh, and he was weak then. My sons could overthrow his army with their toys.'

Cambyses laughed. This was a promising start. 'How best should we enter Egypt?' he asked this man who had once been a general for the pharaoh.

'The desert is largely unguarded', Phanes told him, 'but the sun and the sands are their own guardians. We must ally with Bedouin nomads. They know the desert, and can take us on a route with plenty of food and water for the army.' Cambyses agreed with Phanes's assessment, and sent emissaries to make an alliance with the nomads. The alliance was quickly agreed, and soon the nomads were leading a massive Persian army – including their legendary Immortals, the Emperor's personal guard – across the desert and into Egypt.

The pharaoh, Psamtik III, knew he was in trouble. His Greek allies had been deserting him for some time, and now his border scouts had brought news that a Persian army was approaching. He was not going to give up his kingdom too easily, however. When the Assyrians had helped put his ancestors on the throne, they had also brought improvements in chariot-making and superior *khopesh* swords. He knew that the chariots were very fast and stable shooting platforms, and that his mobile archers were his best hope to keep the Persians out.

He also had something else up his sleeve, which he hoped would turn things around: the two sons of Phanes were caught and held hostage. Psamtik sent spies to the Persian army to meet secretly with Phanes. 'We have your sons,' the Egyptian told Phanes. 'If you would change sides again, and help us drive off the Persians, we will shower them with gold. If not, we will kill them.' This blackmail did not impress Phanes, who knew he'd be killed if he so much as took a step away from the service of Cambyses.

Soon, the Persians massed before the gates of the city of Pelusium, where Psamtik and his army were waiting. Psamtik was frantic by now, and had Phanes's sons brought out to the top of the wall. In a last desperate attempt to distract Phanes from taking part on Cambyses' side, Psamtik had the boys' throats cut in front of their father. The blood was drained into a bowl and

CAMBYSES – OUTRAGE OR OPEN ARMS?

The Greek writer Herodotus describes Cambyses looting palaces, deliberately defiling temples, slaughtering the sacred Apis Bull, and generally trampling all over the society he had just taken over. Herodotus was called the Father of History by the Roman writer Cicero, and the Father of Lies by a lot of others. At one time, it was said that he included too much fantasy in his histories, but now he has been somewhat rehabilitated. So, was he lying or not?

Herodotus was writing only 75 years after Cambyses died, but he was Greek, and at this time the Persian Empire was Greece's main enemy. Propaganda in his writings was a political necessity. In other words, he had to show a leader of the 'bad guys' doing bad things.

We do, however, also have the autobiography of an Egyptian priest, Udjahorusnet, who lived through Cambyses' rule, and was one of his advisers. We know from his writings that both native Egyptian nobles, Jews, Libyans, and other minorities all welcomed the new ruler. Udjahorusnet also tells us that Cambyses went out of his way – at least before his campaigns started going horribly wrong – to avoid offending Egyptian sensibilities.

mixed with wine, from which all the Egyptian soldiers drank. Psamtik had hoped this would drive Phanes wild with fear and grief, and cause him to take his mercenaries out of the invading army and flee. He had misjudged the mercenary, however, who was instead driven to a greater fury and thirst for revenge. Phanes led his men in the spearhead of the attack, backed up by the dreaded and unbeaten Immortals.

Chariots swarmed forward from each army, looping around their enemies and shooting arrows into the crowds of running warriors. As Psamtik had hoped, his chariots were faster and more stable to shoot from, but the brave charioteers were simply outnumbered. Persian archers brought down the horses, while spearmen finished off the charioteers. Cambyses then ordered his Immortals into the fray, and they charged into the mass of Egyptian defenders around the city. The Egyptians were no match for the Immortals, who hacked and slashed with wild abandon, slaughtering the defenders. Swords and axes smashed through wooden spear-hafts and Egyptian flesh with equal ease, and the city was firmly in Persian hands by the end of the day. The lands outside were paved with skulls, as, according to the Greek physician Ctesias, fifty thousand Egyptians and seven thousand Persians died that day.

Psamtik himself, however, had fled almost as soon as the battle began, and Cambyses soon left the battlefield as well, in hot pursuit. Cambyses chased Psamtik all the way to the city of Memphis, at the heart of the Nile Delta. There, Psamtik gathered his personal bodyguard around him, but they were few in number, and the army had already been smashed at Pelusium. It was

(Opposite) When Cambyses took over Egypt, he made sure that he was crowned as pharaoh by all the traditional rituals and ceremony – which included being anointed by priests of Set and Horus, who wore headdresses representing their respective gods.

Egyptian heavy infantryman of the 19th Dynasty, c.1250 BC by Angus McBride. (Osprey Publishing)

easy for Cambyses to break down the gates of Psamtik's palace, kill his guards, and put the pharaoh in chains. Since Psamtik had been a weak king, with little support from his people, there was not much resistance.

In fact, the Egyptians were quite happy to see a stronger leader as pharaoh. Cambyses wanted to keep things that way, and so he made sure to show respect to Egyptian ways. His coronation as pharaoh was conducted in the traditional way, in which he was anointed with oils by priests dressed as the various gods. He was flanked by priests dressed as Horus and Set, and had carvings made showing him blessed by the pair. Soon, Cambyses returned to his own capital of Susa, dragging Psamtik in chains. There, he executed the former pharaoh. He was not done with Egypt yet, however, and remained in the role of pharaoh. Some parts of the country were very remote and had little contact with the capital, so they needed to know who was now in charge. Egypt also had other enemies, who were now enemies of the Persian Empire, and Cambyses was determined to show them that his will was law.

Made confident by his conquest of Egypt, Cambyses decided to lead an army of Persians, Egyptians, and mercenaries south along the Nile into Nubia. This campaign did not go as well. Without local nomads to show them where to find food and water, they soon ran out of both. Without even meeting their enemy, the army was reduced to cannibalism to survive as it crawled home. Next he sent fifty thousand men west into the desert in search of the Siwa oasis. Somewhere along the route, a huge sandstorm blew up and enfolded his struggling army. First blinded, then buried, not a single man of that army was ever seen again. Finally, he planned to invade Carthage, but was enraged and embarrassed when his Phoenician ship captains refused to attack the city that their own families had founded. With each of these defeats and embarrassments, Cambyses became less popular with his subjects, and he was also under threat at home. After only three years as pharaoh, he died in disgrace. Some say he was murdered by ambitious underlings or by his family, while others say he accidentally stabbed himself while mounting his horse.

With Cambyses dead, there was a brief rebellion by some of the Egyptian nobility, but this was quickly crushed by the Persians and their new ruler, Darius. Egypt would then be ruled at a distance from Persia, until Alexander the Great defeated the Persian Empire and began the Ptolemaic dynasty that would lead to Cleopatra.

Weapons and Tactics of Ancient Egypt

Warfare between the gods, as between men, used a wide range of weapons known to the Egyptians. The gods, despite their innate powers, still used spears, axes and *khopeshes*, albeit larger and grander than the weapons used by their mortal allies and followers. They were the same weapons that the armies of Psamtik and Cambyses also used, and, of course, were the same weapons that Thoth magically strengthened to aid Horus's followers. These weapons and their tactics would be used in the same fashion by the followers of the rival gods as they would by the armies of history.

The *khopesh* was essentially a sickle-shaped sword, with the edge on the outside. Because they were usually made of bronze or copper, they were normally cast in a mould, rather than forged by a smith. Although it is the most recognizable of Ancient Egyptian weapons, the *khopesh* originated in Canaan and Mesopotamia, where it had a much longer handle and was used as a kind of war axe. When brought to Egypt it was adapted to single-handed use, as Egyptian soldiers both by training and preference used a wicker shield in one hand and a single-handed weapon in the other.

The *khopesh* was primarily a slashing weapon, and the curvature of the blade meant that, upon impact, a greater pressure was exerted on the target than would be delivered by a straight edge. The blade was thicker and heavier than a straight-bladed equivalent would have been. Normal procedure would have been for a soldier to defend himself with his shield, while using the *khopesh* either in wide cuts at the enemy's body, or to strike at the head as he would use a mace.

Because copper and bronze are relatively soft metals, the thick edge of a *khopesh* could be blunted easily, and it is therefore unlikely that a *khopesh* would have been used to block or parry blade-to-blade. However, the design does include features clearly intended to make the weapon more versatile in combat. The tip is weighted and in line with the hilt and base of the blade, so it was perfectly possible to thrust or jab at an opponent's face. The non-sharpened inside of the curve, if the weapon was reversed or dual-wielded, could be used to catch an opponent's arm or weapon and deflect it. Prior to the New Kingdom's straighter-bladed variant, the weighted tip also had a rear-facing spur, which could hook the edge of an enemy's shield and pull it away, thus exposing him to attack. The *khopesh* fell out of common use in the early 12th century BC, as it was superseded by straight swords introduced to Egypt by the Sea Peoples.

Chariots came to Egypt, like so much military technology, from the Hyksos. By 1500 BC, the pharaoh had over a thousand of them at his command. The Egyptians wanted a lightweight, manoeuvrable chariot for fast strikes – essentially to do the job that mounted cavalry would do much later – but using archers from a mobile shooting platform. This was a two-man vehicle drawn by two horses, carrying a driver and archer. It was a D-shaped wooden

A modern replica of a *khopesh*, which the author has used in re-enactment. (Author's Collection)

Rameses the Great shooting from a (driverless!) chariot in a relief from the temple at Abu Simbel. (PRISMA ARCHIVO / Alamy)

platform, usually sycamore, with a waist-high railing around the front and sides. For war, wooden walls were fitted, sometimes with laminated leather or gilded decoration, to stop arrows or spears from getting through to the occupants.

Where other societies' chariots had an axle in the centre of the floor, the Egyptians put it directly under the rear edge. This meant that the body of the chariot wouldn't tip back and forward as it went over bumps, and would remain a stable platform from which to shoot arrows. The war chariot would have two quivers for arrows slung from the sides at the rear, and a sheath for bows and one for javelins slung from the sides nearer the front. The Egyptian chariot was remarkably lightweight, weighing perhaps as little as 35kg, and could be lifted by one man alone, for example to right the vehicle if it had been overturned. This made it faster than the heavier chariots of the Hittites or other enemies.

The Egyptians used chariots for two main purposes. Firstly, they would protect the vital infantrymen by engaging enemy chariots. The lighter, faster

Egyptian chariots would charge down the oncoming enemy chariots and pass between them. They could then loop round and engage each enemy chariot from the rear, as the heavier enemy vehicles could neither outrun nor out-turn them. Secondly, they were used as fast hit-and-run forces to stake out enemy units most dangerous to the infantry, such as archers. The typical strategy would be to send a stream of chariots towards the enemy group being targeted, and have the archers aboard shoot as rapidly as possible into the enemy while the driver wheeled the chariot in a tight turn before the enemy, in order to get out of the way of the next chariot in the stream behind him. The chariots could then retreat, loop round and repeat the attack until they ran out of arrows, or turn back to make a similar attack on another part of the enemy force. Afterwards, the chariots could harry retreating forces with any remaining arrows or with spears.

Modern tests have shown that a squadron of around fifty Egyptian chariots wheeling in front of an enemy force for the archers to shoot at could unleash up to a thousand arrows a minute onto a specific grouping of the enemy. This is not much less than the rate of fire delivered by the chain-gun on a modern AH-64 Apache helicopter gunship.

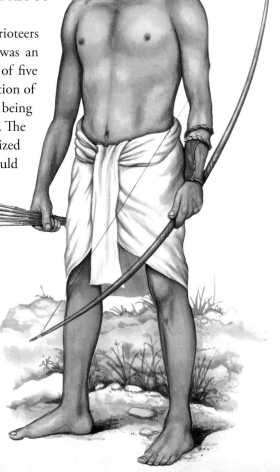

Egyptian Archer from the Middle Kingdom 2055-1650 BC by Peter Bull. (Osprey Publishing)

What is perhaps most interesting is that the charioteers became a new class of their own. Being a charioteer was an expensive business, as one had to pay for the upkeep of five servants, the horses, and the vehicle. This led to the creation of a slightly more aristocratic class of Egyptian warrior, and being a charioteer was seen as socially and politically significant. The chariots were also followed by chariot runners, specialized infantrymen not unlike later panzer-grenadiers. These would run along behind the chariots during engagements with enemy chariots, finish off wounded enemy charioteers, and destroy their vehicles while the Egyptian chariots wheeled. They would also recover fallen Egyptian weapons or personnel.

By the first millennium BC, horse-borne cavalry had largely replaced the chariot in Egyptian warfare.

The first Egyptian bows, as elsewhere in the world, were horn bows, made from antelope horns with a wooden section in the middle. By the beginning of Dynastic times, recurve bows made entirely of wood had replaced horn. During the Old Kingdom, the recurve bow was largely abandoned in favour of the simple bow, now known as the self bow. This was a two-metre-long wooden bow, made of acacia wood and slightly curved at both ends. The self bow remained in use with the Egyptian military throughout the Middle and New Kingdoms, even though composite bows had been introduced by the Hyksos, and recurve bows had returned.

The Hyksos bow brought horn and sinew back to Egyptian archery. It was a recurved bow, shortened and with a pre-existing tension in the wood. Horn, which could take compression, supported the side of the bow facing the archer, while sinew, which could stretch, was bonded to the wood on the side facing the enemy, the whole thing then secured with bark. All of this meant that it had a lot more power and a higher draw weight, in a bow only three to four feet long. The complexity also made the compound bow more difficult to produce and to maintain.

Because re-stringing the compound bow was often a two-man job, it was more common to issue these weapons to chariot archers. The extra power of this bow was a useful frontline weapon against enemies in scale armour, and Egyptian chariots were used for fast archery attacks on targeted areas, so they needed the stronger weapon. The driver could then also assist the archer in re-stringing.

Archers on foot retained the simple self bow throughout the New Kingdom. These were simpler to mass produce, required less maintenance by the infantry, and were used against unarmoured infantry and fleeing enemies.

Different types of arrows were used by Egyptian archers for different purposes. The arrow shaft was made of reed, with three feathers and an arrowhead. The basic arrowhead was flint, with two trailing barbs, although other types of stone and even wooden arrowheads were used alongside these. By the second millennium BC, bronze arrowheads had been introduced, and these were effective when shot from a composite bow in piercing scale armour. Later, barbed iron arrowheads were not unknown, though iron remained a relatively rare and precious metal in Egypt. There were even blunt arrowheads for practice-shooting, and bird-hunting.

In pre-Dynastic times, through to the Old Kingdom, Egyptian soldiers wore only a linen kilt and carried a shield. The blazing sun of Egypt made the wearing of true armour almost unbearably hot, but as Egypt's enemies began to wield better weapons, the need for some form of proper armour arose.

The most common type of protection worn by Egyptian soldiers was not really much in the way of armour; two wide bands of leather crossed the chest and back. This provided a little protection from reed arrows, but was more useful for fending off glancing cuts from knives. This type of armour could be worn by any soldier, but was most commonly seen worn by charioteers, perhaps as protection against small stones thrown upward by the wheels.

Starting around the reign of Amenhotep II, scale armour of Persian design began to be used by elite units, eventually becoming more widespread as the New Kingdom went on. This was incorporated into the Egyptian military while there was a stronger Asiatic influence on the kingdom, as well as being taken from defeated enemies. Scale armour was made from scales of hardened leather or bronze attached to a linen or soft leather tunic. This type of armour is effective against arrows and descending blows, but soldiers quickly learned to strike upwards with daggers or thrusting swords to penetrate a line of scales.

Plate armour, though used elsewhere in the regions surrounding the Mediterranean, was never used in Egypt, simply because large sheets of metal were heated up too much by the sun. There would have been a real danger of wearers being burned by their own armour. This problem also applied to metal helmets, but some bronze helmets have been found in Egypt. These are thought by archaeologists to have been worn by foreign mercenaries, or to be plunder taken from defeated enemies.

Most Egyptians preferred not to wear headgear in general, but helmets were sometimes used in war. The ordinary soldier relied on his hair to protect him. It would be oiled and twisted into tight braids or curls in the hope of at least partly cushioning any glancing blows, though the efficacy of this is debatable, to say the least. Helmets made of wood and ivory platelets were sometimes worn by mercenaries, or by soldiers who had looted them from fallen opponents. The Sherden, fighting as mercenaries, wore helmets decorated with the horns and a solar disc associated with Hathor.

Other forms of armour, such as greaves and breastplates, were not used in Ancient Egypt, but gauntlets were used by charioteers. These were made of thick leather, and intended mostly to provide extra grip on the reins. Some surviving gauntlets, however, have a thick enough back to turn a knife blade, and possibly even a weak strike from a sword.

The original cutting axe from the Old Kingdom was retained, but alongside it the Middle Kingdom Egyptians introduced a new Hyksos-originated weapon, the penetrative axe. This was a single-handed weapon, with a cast metal head of bronze or copper attached to a short haft of around 20-30 inches.

In other kingdoms of the era, axe-heads were cast with an 'eye' through the back of the blade so that the haft could be fitted into it directly. In Egypt, it was attached by means of a mortise and tenon fitting and then secured more tightly by being tied on by leather thongs. In some ways this can be seen as a step backwards, towards the way in which stone or flint axe-heads were attached to their hafts in Neolithic times, but it also meant that the soldier in the field could maintain or replace the axe-head without any metalworking skills.

As the *khopesh* had evolved from a cutting axe into a single-handed weapon by adding a handgrip to the long curved blade, so the penetrative axe became a single-handed weapon by having the blade compressed and attached to a much shorter haft. This meant that the soldier was free to use a shield in his other hand, or indeed to dual-wield two axes.

The axe was usually deployed against an enemy force that was broken or fleeing after taking casualties from archery or spears. In this, and in the

(Overleaf) Of course, mere mortals have always fought each other, and in 525 BC, Egypt's armies clashed with the Persian army of Cambyses II. The Persians, besides superior numbers, had the advantage of being led by a former commander of the pharaoh's army, the Greek mercenary, Phanes.

execution of prisoners, it replaced the mace. An excellent close-combat weapon, the axe could also be used to foul or pull away an enemy's shield, and could easily split a helmet or shield of the era. The axe eventually fell into disuse as the *khopesh* and its straight-bladed successors took over as the infantry's close-combat weapon of choice. Eventually, after the 18th Dynasty, the battle axe was almost entirely reduced to being a ceremonial weapon.

As well as being an excellent weapon for engaging armoured enemies, the penetrative axe could be used for non-combat purposes such as felling trees, or butchery. As with all things Egyptian, ritual and ceremonial versions were developed for royal wear, with extensive artwork on the head. There are many bas-reliefs of pharaohs preparing to smite prisoners with this type of axe, although for some reason the artistic form of the time always has the edge turned away from the victim, as if he is about to be struck with the back or haft rather than the edge.

The most distinctive Egyptian shield, seen in many tomb paintings, scrolls, and wooden models, was the rectangular shield, five feet high, with straight edges on three sides and a pointed arch on top. These shields were basically wooden, some solid flat boards with cowhide leather held down on the outer surface; others were merely frames across which cowhide had been stretched. Amusingly, paintings and surviving models show that the shields were painted with the blotchy patterns of the cowhides from which they came.

These smaller shields could also be carried by a chariot archer when not shooting, but there was no room on an Egyptian chariot for a separate shield-bearer, so the driver and archer would have to rely on their rate of shooting to keep enemies at bay when actually in combat.

This type of shield was useful to protect spear-carrying soldiers from reed arrows and the like, as the soldier could stop and crouch behind it, totally hiding himself. However, the size of the shield made it unwieldy to use for blocking against swords or axes in close-quarter combat. Some soldiers were deployed along with the archers as shield-bearers, to keep the archers on their side covered from arrows or slingshot stones launched by the enemy.

Egyptian military encampments were ringed with these shields, propped up. This kept animals out, horses in, and would clatter when falling if anyone entered the camp. It also meant the men's shields were always ready to be taken up at a moment's notice.

In the second millennium BC, Egypt began to use smaller, more manoeuvrable weapons such as swords and penetrative axes, and to face enemies who used them. This meant that a soldier needed to be able to manoeuvre his shield in order to block with it and protect himself more quickly and with more agility than the old shields would allow. So the cowhide shield was made smaller, and the arched top made into a wider curve. Round shields were carried by the Sea Peoples, some of whom fought for Egypt as mercenaries after the time of Rameses III.

Metal shields were also known, but were more for ceremonial use by the king, as they were less practical as defensive equipment. Because wood and leather are compressible, where bronze is not, they could take impacts from arrows, spears or swords without breaking. Bronze shields were more brittle, and could be split completely by a blow from a *khopesh*.

ENDURING LEGACY

Egyptian Mythology: Purpose and Relevance

Like most of the world's religions, Egyptian mythology served a mixture of purposes. It told stories that attempted to explain the mysteries of creation, showed how much the gods were like people, and also how different from mortals they were. Unlike many of the world's mythologies, however, Egyptian mythology was also designed to lead by example. Thus much of Egyptian life was dedicated to preparing for death and afterlife, and its mythology – in the forms of various funeral texts – reflects this by being a guide to how people

A section of the *Book of the Dead* showing Osiris presiding over the weighing of the heart. (The Art Archive / Alamy)

should prepare. The oldest religious texts in the world, the Pyramid Texts, Coffin Texts (so called because they were painted inside pyramids and on coffins), and *Book Of Going Forth By Day* – better known as the *Book Of The Dead* – were illustrated guidelines and spells designed to give the deceased the correct responses and answers to the tests they would face in the Duat, and taught the deceased's relatives how to help him or her get through the trials of the underworld.

This is certainly the element of the mythology that has most survived to the present day, but it is not all that was intended. Of course, we do not know what messages failed to survive, because they are lost, and we no longer have the context that the Ancient Egyptians had. We can see some other fragments, though. As one example, a story like this one about crossing the Duat deals with the temperaments of animals, warning those living near rivers that hippopotami are to be treated with caution even though they are not carnivorous creatures.

Likewise, on a practical level, the story of the death and resurrection of Osiris included a guide to preserving the deceased for their journey, in the form of mummification. So, what of the actual rivalry between Set and Horus afterwards? Is this just an exciting story, or did it have a real-world relevance to the Egyptians of the time?

The fact that the pair are each in charge of one half of the country indicates that there is a political side to their story: for the country to be whole, both are needed. Two opposing political parties or religious interpretations need to work together. That is a fairly obvious reading, especially considering the nature of Egypt as two linked lands – Upper and Lower Egypt – with their own central versions of the local religion, based in Thebes and Heliopolis respectively, but there is also a more direct practical message in the tale of the strife between Set and Horus.

This part of the surviving mythology can be viewed in the form of an example or guide for Egyptian society in how to conduct formal affairs. When viewed in this light, the myth has some interesting advice for royalty. At the heart of the story, the brother of a dead ruler and the son of that ruler contest the line of succession. They fight over it, they argue over it, they try to each score political points over it, and they appeal to higher authority – the Ennead, the council of the gods – about it, and that higher authority makes it clear that, in the end, the son must inherit. This is very important to the smooth line of succession, especially in a society which, as in Ancient Egypt, claims that the pharaoh is also a god. The myth makes sure that everybody knows that although a brother may be given part of a kingdom, when the true ruler dies his son must take over, no matter what. There were historical instances in which pharaohs appointed relatives as regents, especially while away on campaign, and so some might think that if the pharaoh never returned the regent would keep the throne. However, this particular story tells us that once

the reigning monarch is officially dead, his son (assuming there is one) must take over, and that the regent must give up the throne. Daughters and sisters are not even considered, making it a male lineage.

Is this what the story was meant to tell the Ancient Egyptians? Nobody knows for sure, but it would be strange indeed if none of them ever thought about it that way.

Then and Now

The story of Set and Horus has had a long legacy, which continues down to the present day. In fact it has several legacies, from various different elements of the myth. The murder of Osiris, followed by his resurrection (a section of the myth which is sometimes viewed as a separate story altogether) can still be seen in later religions.

Both Greeks and Romans assimilated the religions of other territories they absorbed, and Egypt was no exception. When the Greeks ruled Egypt, they equated their gods with the Greek gods, and vice versa. Set, as we saw earlier,

The Eye of Horus, sometimes called the Eye of Ra, was an Ancient Egyptian symbol of protection and good health.

was equated with Typhon, while Osiris was equated with Zeus, the king of the gods, Horus with Apollo, and so on.

Some historians and writers have suggested that the story of Jesus's resurrection might even be a take on the resurrection of Osiris, though the circumstances are very different, as Osiris could only 'live' in the underworld. Nevertheless, it is true that Osiris dies in order to show everyone else the way to immortality (in the form of mummification). The Copts who continued the rituals of mummification into the 8th century AD certainly interpreted the preparation by Joseph of Jesus's body in its shroud as being intended as a form of mummification, according to St Augustine. More directly, the usual depiction of Isis holding the infant Horus led quite smoothly to the first millennium's imagery of the Madonna and Child, in the artistic style of late Roman paintings.

Isis, of all the deities in the story, is the one whose influence and worship lasted the longest and spread the furthest, probably because of her universal appeal as wife and mother. Everyone in every culture understands those roles, and so the attributes of Isis spread quickly and widely all around the Mediterranean, and, eventually, beyond. Plutarch actually wrote his version of the story as a letter to a Greek high priestess of Isis in his time.

One other way in which this Egyptian tale has possibly influenced popular Christianity is in the basic idea of an enemy of the main god, whether that be the opposite of god (the devil) or of Jesus (the Antichrist). The diametric opposition between Horus and Set could be interpreted as similar to the way most people imagine the Antichrist to be the opposite of Jesus. On a related note, Set still has an official religion, though it has nothing much to do with Ancient Egyptian beliefs. In 1975, a splinter group from the Church of Satan

started up the Temple of Set in California, which still exists today.

This connection between modern religions brings up a common suggestion; that 'Satan' is a variation on the name 'Set'. This is not the case, however, as the name 'Satan' derives from a Hebrew word meaning 'the opposer', while the name 'Set' is merely one of several possible pronunciations of the Egyptian word 'swt'. Egyptian hieroglyphics did not record vowels, and so the pronunciation of words and names is open to interpretation. 'Set' is the Coptic version of the name, while 'Seth' was the Greek. Modern archaeologists think – but are far from certain – that it was most likely originally pronounced 'sutak' or 'sutal'.

On a simpler note, the tale of the two brothers vying for the crown is a timeless story. The sibling rivalry element alone is a fixture of tales from the Biblical Cain and Abel through to modern epics like *Game Of Thrones*. Likewise, the murdered rightful king being followed by first a usurper and then a vengeful prince is a story found in every culture on the planet. It is the plot of quite a few Shakespeare plays, for example. Take *Hamlet*: the king's brother murders him for the throne, and the son of the dead king – who meets his late father 'resurrected' as a ghost in a sheet – comes back to reclaim the throne. Sound familiar?

A 13th century Byzantine-style Madonna and child. Of all the characters in the myth, Isis may have got the best deal where longevity of her image is concerned. (Robert Estall photo agency / Alamy)

Here is another one: the golden-haired son of a figure who was chopped to pieces before being resurrected in a special set of wrappings in the darkness, and goes on a quest with magical aid from a wiser man, which eventually leads to him confronting the once apparently good schemer who was ultimately responsible for destroying the father in order to seize a throne. Or, as most people call it, the *Star Wars* franchise. True, it mixes up the different symbolic figures and elements, but they are all there.

Essentially, Horus's search for justice over Set is the archetypal hero's journey that the mythologist Joseph Campbell promoted. It certainly includes most of the tropes he lists as being elements of that journey: a villainous father figure, reconciliation with the real father, journeys to the underworld, failure

(Opposite) Isis nursing Horus in a statue from the Louvre. (The Art Archive / Alamy)

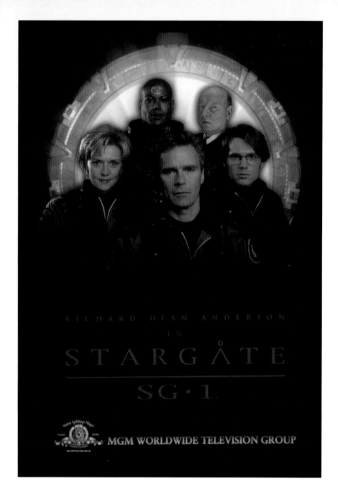

Many of the Egyptian gods, including Apep, Osiris and Set, appeared as villains in the *Stargate* TV series. (Bureau L.A. Collection/Sygma/Corbis)

of the first battle, a series of challenges, magical aid, a dead mentor, and so on.

Many gods and elements of these myths have continued to be fascinating to modern writers and filmmakers. For example, Horus appears, along with Thoth, Anubis and Bast, in Neil Gaiman's novel *American Gods*, but Set is only referenced in passing. Surprisingly, considering how rooted in Egyptian mythology the franchise is, neither Horus nor Set have played that big a part in *Stargate*. Ra, of course, appeared in the original movie as an alien who had possessed a shepherd boy from Ancient Egypt, but the spin-off TV series, *Stargate SG1* was replete with gods and goddesses from Egyptian mythology and beyond, who were in fact alien parasites in human host bodies. Set appears only in one episode, 'Seth' in season three, in which it is revealed that he stayed on earth for thousands of years, and ended up the leader of a small cult of about a dozen people. This is pretty odd, given the need to be worshipped of both the mythological gods and *Stargate*'s alien Goa'uld – you would think after thousands of years of being the only actual (faux) deity living on earth he would have a bigger influence, and lead a major world religion, whether a real one or one created for the show.

Horus did not appear in the series at all, though the character of Heru'ur is named for the Greek name for Horus the Elder. Apep, under his Greek name Apophis, was the recurring villain for the first couple of seasons of the show. Osiris did briefly appear as the only male Goa'uld with a female host, cleverly evoking the idea from the myth of his genitalia having never been recovered. As a judge of the dead and figure of resurrection, Osiris was also frequently referenced in *Buffy The Vampire Slayer*, usually in connection with reviving the dead.

In the world of Robert E. Howard's character Conan the Barbarian, there is a character called Set, who is an evil snake-god, clearly taking his cue from the later Greek tellings of the myths, in which all of Apep's attributes are given to Set. This serpentine version of Set is also a villain in the video game *Sphinx And The Cursed Mummy*, and he also took on Lara Croft in *Tomb Raider - The Last Revelation*.

Set's finest hour – albeit as a character of pure evil – in modern media comes in the 1975 *Doctor Who* story *Pyramids Of Mars*, in which, going by the more

The Mummy Returns

It was not just the Osiris-worshipping Ancient Egyptians who were fond of mummification in Egypt. As Egypt was successively ruled by Persians, Greeks, and Romans, the temptation to be preserved for eternity continued to spread. In fact, there were more people looking to be mummified in these later periods than ever before.

Originally, in the earlier dynasties, the mummification process was reserved for the pharaoh, who would become Osiris. As the united Egypt grew and prospered, so mummification became the ultimate fate for royal families, nobles, high priests, and eventually anyone who wanted and could afford it. This led to a problem: there was not enough natron to go round, which meant that other, cheaper materials began to be used as well, such as bitumen. In fact the word 'mummy' comes from *mumia*, the Arabic word for a thing of bitumen. Worse still, there were not enough trained and experienced embalmers to go round, which meant a lot of mummies started to be made by what a modern person might call 'cowboy' embalmers. They used the wrong materials, which meant the deceased would rot rather than being preserved as intended, and indeed were often more damaged in the process. Even the spells and amulets to protect and guide the deceased in the Duat frequently went terribly wrong, as by the Graeco-Roman era hieratic had replaced hieroglyphics as Egypt's language, and many of these cowboy embalmers could not read or write the hieroglyphs, so they made mistakes, such as sticking in totally random spells and getting the name – and even gender – of the deceased wrong. Osiris and Anubis must have been very confused when some of these turned up.

Between these problems, and the fact that more and more of the mummies were of people from different cultures and religions than the Ancient Egyptian one, the exterior decoration of the mummies became more important than spells and amulets and the like. Death masks and decoration that showed off the status of the deceased became more prevalent. In the region around Faiyum, which was on the site of the oldest settlement in Egypt, a form of pigmented wax painting was used to paint portraits on boards tied to the heads of mummies. This practice continued throughout the Roman occupation and all the way into the Christian era.

Of course, Christians had no interest in having portraits of ancient pagan gods painted on their bodies, and so their portraits were almost photo-realistic images of the deceased as they had been in life. The Coptic Christians believed in mummification because they thought that angels would ensure that the body of the dead would be raised incorruptible, as that of Jesus had been. Mummification gave them a head start in this, and so it remained a part of Coptic Christianity until well into the 8th century AD. By this point, little of the actual process of mummification was retained. In the 7th and 8th centuries AD, bodies no longer had their organs removed for drying, but were simply wrapped in salt and linen with generally unsuccessful results.

An example of the fine portraiture on a Roman-era Coptic mummy. (The Print Collector / Alamy)

accurate pronunciation of Sutekh, he is revealed to be an alien from a planet called Phaester Osiris who would end all life in the cosmos, but who had been imprisoned by Horus. In this version, Horus was his brother, suggesting that this Horus was Horus the Elder. Horus does not appear, though his voice – performed by the same actor as plays Sutekh – is heard.

It will never end. It cannot, as long as people still tell stories, because this is one of the oldest stories there is, except that it never gets old. The names may change, and the attributes of the characters may vary, but the story will never truly be forgotten, because not only is it a universal story that has gone far beyond its original cultural context, but because the people who told it and wrote it down did that so well.

Plutarch might have given us a version with a very different Set from the character that the ancients probably intended, but in the end he probably did Set a favour, because he is the character who is most memorable. Osiris's role in the story was to be the archetypal mummy, but mummification is not a going concern today. Horus showed the Egyptians that the son of the pharaoh should inherit the throne, but there are no more pharaohs. Set was never intended to be the embodiment of all evil, but audiences love to have a villain to boo, and, in becoming that villain, Set became the most remembered of them all. Maybe Horus did not really win after all.

The Eyes of Horus look down over the Eyptians at work in this bas-relief sculpture. (Library of Congress)

SELECT BIBLIOGRAPHY

Clayton, Peter A., *Chronicle Of The Pharaohs*, Thames & Hudson (1994)

Herodotus, *Histories*, Penguin Classics (1959)

Meeks, Dmitri, and Favard-Meeks, Christine, *Daily Life Of The Egyptian Gods*, John Murray (1997)

Partridge, Robert P., *Fighting Pharaohs: Weapons And Warfare In Ancient Egypt*, Peartree Publishing (2002)

Plutarch, *Essays*, trans. Robin Waterfield, Penguin Classics (1992)

Rosalie, David, *Religion And Magic In Ancient Egypt*, Penguin (2000)

Shaw, Ian, *Oxford History Of Ancient Egypt*, Oxford University Press (2000)

Silverman, David P., *(ed.), Reference Classics: Ancient Egypt*, Duncan Baird Publishers (2003)

Wilkinson, Richard H., *The Complete Gods And Goddesses Of Ancient Egypt*, Thames & Hudson (2003)

Wise, Terence, *Men At Arms: Ancient Armies Of The Middle East*, Osprey Publishing (1981)